GW01081223

OPENING THE INNER-MIND

FROM JOE (FLAT ①)

MY FIRST BOOK
ON GURDJIEFF

OPENING THE INNER-MIND

VOLUME ONE

'Holy-affirming, holy-denying, holy-reconciling,
transubstantiate in me, for my being.'

META-PSYCHOLOGY
—— AND ——
THE MASTERS OF WISDOM

ADVANCED LEVEL ESOTERIC MATERIALS

BY MR J. McKEANEY

ESOTERIC TEACHER

Published under licence by Brown Dog Books and
The Self-Publishing Partnership, 7 Green Park Station, Bath BA1 1JB

www.selfpublishingpartnership.co.uk

ISBN printed book: 978-1-78545-214-7
ISBN e-book: 978-1-78545-215-4

Cover design by Kevin Rylands

Printed and bound by CPI Group (UK) Ltd, Croydon CR0 4YY

The Core Teaching

Preliminary Work and Exploration of Esoteric Materials:

A CONCISE FOURTH WAY PRIMER

THE WORKSHOPS

An opportunity to engage with high-level esoteric teachings and change your cognitive level: going beyond culture-bound reasoning and narrow 'educational' modalities... structures which only serve to retard those cognitive abilities in the first place. There is no theoretical limit to what you can achieve – with esoteric wisdom, you enter a new paradigm of higher learning and a portal to a new world you never thought possible.

N.B.
These manuals are made available to those participating in esoteric workshops and those few individuals who have the cognitive range to understand and appreciate profound and arcane esoteric principles.

Warning: These materials are of a particular and unusual nature - they originate not in ordinary society but from the strata of higher-mind or higher Being. I am merely a channel for these potent and arcane principles and ideas - they do not emanate from me. Should you be the type of person who is 'locked into logic' and linear thinking, then these materials may not be suitable for you. These materials begin at a level above logic; in what esotericism calls the psychological-realm. See page 12 for a full explanation of this principle - The Three Minds.

Contact: josephmckeaney@hotmail.com
Website: www.thecoreteaching.weebly.com

GENESIS OF TRUE INTELLIGENCE

'There are some things which you have to do for yourself; these include familiarising yourself with study-materials given to you.

You can only really do this – and thus acquire real qualities, if you suspend the indulgence of desire for immediate satisfactions.'

Sufi Saying [1]

The People of the Path

'YOU CANNOT MANIPULATE THEM –

YOU CANNOT SHUN OR DISTANCE THEM -

YOU CANNOT BENEFIT THEM NOR CAN YOU HARM THEM -

*YOU CANNOT ENNOBLE THEM NOR CAN YOU
DEBASE THEM –*

THEREFORE THEY ARE THE MOST VALUED IN THE WORLD!'

Lau Tzu - *Tao Te Ching* [2]

*'Until a Man Uncovers Himself,
He Cannot See!'*

Gurdjieff

The Three Component Parts of Man's Being: Essence, Personality and the False-Ego!

The Sign

Talk not at all about things sublime and essential.
Seek the level of him whom you speak;
So as not to humble and distress him.
Be frivolous, too, when you are with the frivolous,
But once in a while, as if unsought,
Or even thoughtlessly,
Drop into their cups, on the foam of frivolity
A small petal from the flower of your dreams.

If it is not noticed, recover it cautiously
And always smiling, go your way.
If, however, someone picks up the frail, small petal
And examines it, inhales its fragrance.
Give him forthwith and carefully a sign of discrete understanding.
Then let him behold one of the few of the marvellous flowers of your garden.

Tell him of the invisible divinity which surrounds us all.
And give him the magic word,
The 'Open Sesame' to true freedom.

By A. Nervo – Mexican Poet [3]

The Three Minds

One: <u>The Sensual or Intellectual Mind</u>
Logic. Contemporary science. The five senses. Only believes what is seen or proved by science. Represents a specific mind-set in society... science cannot understand a person who operates from the <u>Inner-Mind</u>! The Sensual Mind is a very limited and deceptive cognitive function! Unable to comprehend real and authentic esoteric wisdom! This level of mind tends to be very egocentric!
(One centred cognition and thinking ... Intellectual Centre)

Two: <u>The Intermediate or Emotional Mind</u>
Belief systems. Emotionalism. The belief in something - religion / creed. Again represents a specific mind-set in society at large. Emotionally centred people cannot understand a person who is centred in the Inner-Mind! Unreliable as a cognitive function – lacks depth and veracity! Naïve views about life and living!
(One centred cognition ... Emotional Centre)

Three: <u>The Inner-Mind</u>
Intuitive awareness combined with emotional centre and intellectual centre. Also called psychological thinking or psychological awareness. The use of three centres simultaneously and, engaging the higher parts of centres.
<u>The Inner-Mind does not accept the conclusions of the Sensual-Mind or the Intermediate-Mind</u>! Represents a new cognitive function in ordinary man!
The Inner-Mind in each of us is vastly superior to either the Sensual-Mind or the Intermediate-Mind. It has higher cognitive powers which the others do not have access to! All initial esoteric work concerns opening this particular inner function in the individual! This function 'opens the perceptions' to the need for prolonged inner-work – it cannot be faked, before those whose Inner-Mind is already opened!
(Three centres working together as an integrated triad)

Introduction

It is a great privilege to introduce the esoteric teachings of George Ivanovitch Gurdjieff in this manual: 'to those who have ears to hear and eyes to see'. I have added small elements from other esoteric lines, where I thought it appropriate! I do hope with all my Being, that you will benefit from the enclosed materials, as I have over the years, and I hope it opens for you a new vision of life and the cosmos; a new awakening. This is indeed, the Golden Path the Great have trod!

The principles and ideas covered in the following pages come to us from esoteric schools – from pre-pharaonic Egypt to be precise. This wisdom so revered by the ancients, comes to us from a time before the pharaohs, before the sands covered ancient Egypt. Gurdjieff tells us: 'This wisdom comes from ancient Egypt, not the one that we know but one that we do not know; it existed in the same place as the other - but it existed much earlier!' We are dealing with a highly sophisticated civilisation which dates to a time before the Pharaonic dynasties – certain artefacts still in existence in today's Egypt come from that period; the Sphinx for example.

The Sphinx has now been calculated to be at least 7,500 years old and possibly as old as 11,500 years old. This calculation has come about, through measuring the erosion caused by precipitation on the surface of this structure; it was not caused by sand say the experts, but by the rainfall of pre-sands Egypt. An astounding discovery! (It is interesting to note that Gurdjieff possessed a map of this period)

This knowledge is not suitable for everyone because it represents a paradigm completely opposed to that which we see all around us in society today! It is the antithesis of all of the false banal cultural activities and pseudo educational modalities which now create such a corrosive effect on the psyche of modern man. Gurdjieff has stressed this point time and time again, when he mentions in his writings 'the abnormal conditions everywhere now encountered by modern man'.

Such is the very nature of esoteric wisdom that it has a very particular effect on the conditioned psyche, and that effect can often be that of negative reactions!

Here I also wish to express my gratitude to all those who have endeavoured to transmit this wisdom to future generations, including Gurdjieff himself – this is a 'karmic-field' which is highly valuable for every truly intelligent human being. I highly recommend reading the works of George I. Gurdjieff, Ouspensky, Maurice Nicoll, John Bennett, Orage and others who were his direct or indirect students. A final word of warning; there are many pseudo-Gurdjieffian groups out there today, claiming his esoteric mantle, most are shoddy fakes – caveat emptor!

A Word of Warning is Necessary Here

Generally speaking, people are highly conditioned entities and, this very same conditioning blocks most individuals from seeing the Truth about the inner-teachings of Man, i.e. esoteric teachings; taking them to be dubious, crafty inventions or the crank formulations of misguided terrestrials.

What one must remember here, is that we tend to exempt ourselves from this set of highly conditioned people. Further, we tend to exempt ourselves from this equation, where we are familiar with New Age or religious materials in general – this is yet another trap for the naive. As we will see later in this No. 1 Volume, being familiar with these basic ideas, in no way prepares us for the reception of genuine, high level esoteric teachings!

Many individuals who have some background in New Age and religious materials do not possess the cognitive level to understand authentic esoteric material. Thus the paradox arises, people with the aforementioned learning or experience, cannot understand esoteric materials yet presume that they can! Not wishing to be viewed as stupid or ignorant – they very often state something akin to the following - 'of course, I understand these ideas... '

This explains why so few terrestrials perceive the real nature and genuine importance of esotericism; it is just beyond their cognitive level! We will discuss the paradox further on, in this current volume.

'The teaching I bring, is completely self-supporting and independent of other spiritual lines, and it has been completely unknown up to the present time!'

G.I. Gurdjieff

CONTENTS

ADVICE FOR THE READER

I strongly advise not reading this transmission of esoteric wisdom in the usual or orthodox way. This material, which contains many esoteric ideas and also principles, brought to us by the incredible Mr Gurdjieff in the last century, should be read several times: three if possible.

This material can be taken as a kind of food for the spirit, a kind of dynamic inner nourishment and also a type of cognitive exercise or spiritual catalyst.

These materials should be 'digested' and not taken in a purely intellectual way. This is where, of course, our emotional function comes into the equation!

This requires time, contemplation and pondering. The essence and origins of these materials do not emanate from me! They come to us from *higher mind*.

It is a mistake to seek immediate satisfactions and/or items, which always confirm your own belief system: an emotional evaluation or link with these materials should be a priority. Normally people only accept that which confirms their own narrow and trite belief system – all else is mentally filtered out of the equation!

The sincere study of esoteric materials can in real terms increase your cognitive range, over time. This forms the true foundation to all authentic inner work. An increase in Being attracts a different external life – one that is more fulfilling, real and substantive. This was the aim of all schools, all religions and all genuine teachings on the Earth – during all epochs.

With real sincerity and careful industry you may come to love the wisdom once held in such esteem and reverence by the ancients of our world. To love this wisdom is to make forever a place in your heart for Truth, vision, courage, and compassion in your very presence; towards all living beings.

Conscious efforts made in the sphere of knowledge and Being are never lost and stay with us permanently, by comparison, all mechanical actions, defective and logical thinking; cynical stances and subsequent results are lost to us forever!

In the beginning, to study oneself and the environment we find ourselves in a position whereby we need to study lying. Ouspensky informs us: 'The psychology of ordinary man is the psychology of lying.' The study of lying in man and in society forms a complete study in itself, within the remit of esoteric work. This study is important because we must recognise lying in ourselves and all of the different categories of lies that inhabit our consciousness. The more we gain insight into this subtle psychology of lying, the more opportunity we evolve to change it. <u>Sincerity is the key</u>!

'Great Knowledge changes destiny!'

Ancient Chinese Proverb [4]

'I saw without hesitation, that in the field of psychology, which I knew better than any other and which I was really able to distinguish the old from the new, the known from the unknown; Gurdjieff knew more than all of European science taken as a whole!'

P.D. Ouspensky

COMMENTS FROM
THE WRITER

Today, we live in a world shattered by low-level mental illness, government lies and manipulation, identity crisis, widespread depression, war, famine and rape.

We have an 'education' system which produces young adults devoid of all the qualities, abilities and emotional development really necessary for reaching the age of majority. Many young people now leave 'education' spoiled, in the real sense of the word, as applied to the psyche of man. They leave, in fact, very imbalanced people, with only training of the intellect and very little else besides!

We could be forgiven for thinking that we are still living in the Dark Ages with the exception of technology, transport and communications, etc – there is little progress with the inner-life of man. In our Being we are still quite primitive – although for modern man, he likes to consider himself highly civilised and cultured; any criticism of his qualities and intelligence hurts his vanity and conceit! To mention modern man's ignorance provokes hostility!

Gurdjieff explains that <u>emotional development</u> is the most important aspect of the human condition, without which there is insecurity, vanity, a lack of identity, the inability to form relationships of substance with others in life, <u>a lack of integrity</u> and a reluctance to give genuine and sincere help to others – without rewards!

He tells us, the core element missing from 'education' today (there are others) is that of the training of the emotional side in the individual.

People are leaving modern 'education' without developing their emotional side, thus we find individuals who may have excellent academic ability but possess the emotional level of a ten year old! I assure you this is no exaggeration! A person may have a very high intellectual capacity but still have a low cognitive level!

It can be safely said that, this remains '<u>a blind-spot</u>' for modern peoples; people are often conscious of the need for academic or intellectual ability but are rarely aware of the need for Being-development. In fact, the collective have no concept of Being or Being-development; this again is the result of a vacuous, arrogant and impoverished mind-set, behind modern 'education'.

This is, of course, the worst possible outcome, because instead of a well-balanced individual reaching adulthood, we find people who are really spoiled. We will find selfishness in place of generosity of spirit, a trite judgmental mind-set instead of compassion, narrow perception where <u>deep insight</u> should be, and <u>answers learned</u>

by rote for all situations. <u>This means that people cease to think for themselves, but rely on borrowed answers – taken ad hoc, from their vacuous culture and shallow 'education' system.</u> This, because it is <u>easier</u> to do it in this fashion, and because Man has 'lost his way'!

When such an individual is placed in a situation outside their normal or habitual environment, we find that they are very often lost; their little list of <u>artificial answers and trite life solutions no longer stand the test of adaptability</u>, without adaptive thinking and resolute and courageous responses, fear and apprehension often enter the equation.

It is only through the maturation of the individual's emotional field, that genuine courage, tenacity and self-confidence manifests for real.

A person who is rounded in their development is a person who not only has experienced much, but also has a 'hands-on' approach to life and all the difficult situations one is bound to encounter. It is not sufficient to 'know', one must also do! <u>It is only through doing that we 'ground' our knowledge and make it real</u>! (Otherwise our 'knowledge' stays in Personality – academia.)

'Children are conceived, very often unwillingly, still more often unintentionally, by people who do not even try to understand the extraordinary event they are bringing about. When children are born they are subjected almost from birth to influences which inevitably produce in them such characteristics as vanity, self-will, self-importance, distrust, deceitfulness, suggestibility, dependence on other people and, at the very root and centre of their being – egoism.

Neglecting the inward life – except by stuffing the child with every kind of absurdity – they do everything possible to establish the conviction that it is what we appear to be, and not what we are, that is important. Children are made to think and to feel, by influences which are brought to bear on them almost from birth, that it is their external manifestations seen by other people, which determine their value.'

John G. Bennett (*What are we living for?*)

BIG MISTAKE NO. 1

'It won't happen to my children!'

Wrong – it is already happening all around you and, you have no control whatsoever over it. Private schools provide no safeguard against the modern psychological contagion of spoiled adolescence! Outwardly your children may appear normal – but they are not! There is much missing in them, which constitutes normality.

BIG MISTAKE NO. 2

'I will send my kids to a holistic school'

Wrong again, although much better than the above approach to education, this provides no barrier to young people adopting the maladjusted thinking and false emotional-anchors prevalent in society at large.

BIG MISTAKE NO. 3

'I will educate my children at home, away from a vacuous and maladapted system of education'

This, although in many ways better than the two previous methods, is not a complete solution. Without knowledge of <u>what a child really needs</u> and without setting an example yourself – results may only prove marginally better than the other routes. Without the education and training of the young person's emotional life, without a developmental praxis for the <u>opening of real qualities</u> in the young person, such as sensitivity, compassion, courage, tenacity, humility, sincerity etc, there is no maturation in the emotional side of an individual. This cannot be achieved without action, i.e. without young people engaging in real life situations and learning through their mistakes.

There is also the training of the young person's actual emotions and the weaning away from the expression of useless negative emotions; spite, bitterness, hate, revenge, ugly verbal expressions of aggression and the useless expenditure of emotional energy in arguments and fights. All of which only serve to reinforce negative traits and habits in the emotional life of the individual – making it more difficult in adulthood to break away from useless negative emotions and also negative life patterns such as swearing, fighting, arguments, worrying, anxiety, insecurity and irrational fears. <u>Qualities must be developed alongside knowledge</u>!

The core of this is that <u>real qualities</u> need to be developed in young people, in a concrete way – this cannot be achieved in the classroom through an academic approach. The huge error is, that today, people think this all happens in the class.

Young people need example and role models who possess these qualities in themselves, modern teachers despite their good intentions and very hard work, do not possess these Essence-qualities; <u>since they themselves are a product of an identical mode of 'education'. Qualities only pass from one person to another</u>! (Another 'blind-spot' in modern cognitive behaviour!)

What can be done? Only what esotericism calls <u>the second education</u> can alter the mind-set and emotional-field of an individual … this will be discussed at length in volume 2 of this series. <u>Qualities cannot be learned – they must be developed</u>! The cognitive ability of modern man precludes this awareness!

THE TEMPORARY SUSPENSION OF OLD THINKING and BELIEF SYSTEMS

It may be apt to mention here, the best way to approach esoteric writings and Knowledge that ultimately have reached us, either directly or indirectly through higher-mind; is not through your habitual modes of thinking and comparison.

Where you wish to give yourself the best chance and opportunity of approaching esoteric teachings, it is imperative that you take on board a few very important principles. In order to approach esoteric wisdom, it is first necessary to suspend old 'hard and fast' modes of thinking, old emotional habits and the hubris that <u>we already know</u>. It is necessary to leave behind culture-bound reasoning and societal conditioning, which almost everyone without exception is subject to!

It is also necessary to suspend judgment* on that which you read in this manual and not seek to measure materials and insights, through the prism of your present 'cognitive lens'. For with persistence and tenacity, it is very possible and also inevitable that your present 'cognitive lens' will enlarge quite dramatically and exponentially over time. In reality, <u>there is much to gain and nothing to lose</u>!

* (Called 'cognitive dissonance' by people today!)

WHAT ARE ESOTERIC TEACHINGS?

It is necessary to begin this volume with a short introduction to esotericism – in order to facilitate those individuals who may pick up this written material, by accident or otherwise and possess very little prior knowledge of this subject.

Gurdjieff tells us that in ancient times, 2,500 BC, in the early Babylonian period of history, people knew the meaning of esotericism. They understood the basic principles involved, and the subject was spoken about openly and commonly on the streets of Babylon itself! They still possessed the requisite cognitive ability! (Awareness)

Today it is a different matter! These principles are now replaced by a vast array of false emotional-anchors and dubious modern day topics such as: football, Olympics, tennis, pornography, cinema, TV, fashion, 'my property', make-up, food, hobbies etc. People no longer possess the cognitive level to perceive the strata of esoteric teachings or, if you like – higher learning!

THE CORE TEACHING

G. tells us that behind orthodox religion, orthodox science and philosophy there is a hidden corpus of knowledge and wisdom on the Earth: a body of knowledge that has always existed in the background and which holds the keys to man's destiny and inner development. This wisdom lies just outside of modern man's cognitive-range - as he is today! What I mean by this, is that, without a definitive adjustment of his cognitive instrument, what one might call a certain cognitive training, he is unable to perceive it! He has now become hypnotised by the flow of material life and lost much cognitive range!

In the movie called 'The Matrix', Morpheus tells Neo: 'Unfortunately nobody can tell you what the Matrix is; you must see it for yourself!' This is precisely the position of modern man in relation to esotericism. In other words – in order to see the existence of 'the Matrix', it is necessary to expand one's cognitive range.

This is the knowledge we will deal with in this volume and in future volumes! G. informs us that the realisation that this hidden aspect of life exists; that is, this initial adjustment of one's cognitive range is the first manifestation of true intelligence in the individual. ('The Matrix' means a society without substance and a modus operandi without a dynamic harmonic structure!)

THE ESOTERIC LEGACY

It is said that a special knowledge, a secret science or Alchemy has existed since the time of Atlantis or before, which has been passed down to contemporary times, through an unbroken chain of initiates; this knowledge, it is said, enables the individual to transcend the limitations of ordinary life and ordinary awareness, by developing a higher level of consciousness or cosmic intelligence.

Fragments of this wisdom may be found in certain types of ancient art, sacred dancing, medieval architecture, certain religious rituals, and ancient scriptures all over planet Earth. It is said that Leonardo da Vinci had just begun decoding some of this ancient knowledge from objective geometry, hidden in the paintings of some of 'the Old Persian Masters', just before he died!

These are the influences, which can be found in a fragmented form in life; but there are also <u>influences of a direct form</u> to be found, where one is re-educated and indeed receive what esotericism terms '<u>the second-education</u>'.

However, to pursue this wisdom requires courage from the individual who is in search of it, since it demands that one goes directly against one's life conditioning and programming from parents and 'education'.

Man's Obligation

'Man's obligation is to co-operate with the laws which operate the Universe. Because man has a unique place, the obligation goes with that ... the awareness of your place is not a gift of nature. You must find it by conscious effort, not by hope. Man has a potentiality he knows nothing about. This forms the science of ancient times. We have lost all idea of these potentialities.'

Gurdjieff [5]

For untold centuries, The Masters of Wisdom (Khawajan) have projected vestiges of this hidden knowledge into society, with the aim of providing a path to true knowledge and initiation; to provide a Core Teaching capable of healing and transforming individuals on a deep transcendent level. This inner work has always been achieved through, firstly, achieving balance and integration in the physical, mental and emotional elements of a person. Although it must be understood that this work of balancing the individual remains, for esotericism, a first step in a long process of inner-development.

'There are a thousand things which prevent a man from awakening, which keep him in the power of his imagination and dreams. In order to act consciously with the intention of awakening, it is necessary to know the forces, which keep man in a state of sleep. First of all, it must be realised that the sleep in which man exists on this earth is not normal, but hypnotic sleep. Man is hypnotised, and this hypnotic state is continually maintained and strengthened in him. One would think that there are forces for whom it is useful and profitable to keep man in a hypnotic sleep state and prevent him from seeing the truth and understanding his position.'

Maurice Nicoll [6]

CHILD OF EARTH

In today's world, naivety rules supreme in relation to religion, cults, modern pharmaceutical medicine, science, art, 'education', advertising etc. This is due to the incredible suggestibility of contemporary man in modern societies.

'One half of the world does not know how the other half lies.'

Gurdjieff

Let us take for example the ideas of some New Age movements versus esoteric teachings: in general, modern people cannot tell the difference!

New Age versus Esoteric Teaching

There is a distinct disjunction between esoteric teaching and New Age ideas.
When we examine both of these modalities ruthlessly, we find some surprising results. What we find is that esoteric teachings stand on a much higher level than New Age ideas, which are founded on the scattered debris of some gigantic whole. We find most New Age teachings are, in fact, belief systems in disguise! Most New Age teachings are based on esoteric ideas!

It has been said that New Age ideas are 'like leaves that have fallen from the esoteric tree'. Gurdjieff tells us that all the scattered teachings we see today, all of the teachings of mini-cults, renegade religions, sects, New Age materials etc, are all fragmented elements from a greater whole: a core teaching which once existed upon the Earth ... the true esoteric teachings of the ancients.

Now, esoteric teachings are not belief systems, unlike religions, cults and New Age teachings. However, it is almost impossible for the modern mind-set to grasp this. Many of the New Age teachings in the modern world have fragments of esoteric teachings at their core – such as the much-vaunted reincarnation and the 'transmigration of the soul'. Despite this, the truth about reincarnation has not been revealed in New Age teachings; they have become diluted and suffered the corrosive effects of the logical mind and generations of wrong thinking on the subject. Gurdjieff explains: 'Everything we get spiritually must be earned.' (This earning includes reincarnation!)

This mode of adopting a fragment of genuine esoteric truth and setting it at the heart of a modern New Age teaching, lends a type of authenticity and veracity to those propagating such a teaching and, of course, as is always the case, many are taken in by this quaint technique. It is <u>this use of a fragment of authentic teaching</u> which we find set amongst the fake ideas of a fertile imagination, that causes all the problems. We find that people will hold onto such teachings 'for grim death'! They become a type of psychological and emotional crutch; in reality a fabrication! <u>Truth is thus sacrificed yet again</u>!

In reality, many New Age and religious teachings <u>actually block inner-work in modern people</u>! <u>Who will do spiritual work if they think that they are going to reincarnate free gratis and without any efforts on their part</u>? The answer is, of course, nobody will do any <u>real spiritual work</u> but merely practice minor spiritual disciplines – <u>practices which were originally used as preparatory items, in much larger and complete Spiritual Paths.</u>

<u>This false idea of reincarnation also stops many balanced and naturally gifted individuals, in the spiritual sphere of life, from looking deeper into genuine esoteric teachings and authentic inner-work … they remain on the periphery.</u>

'Child of Earth, long hast thou dwelt in darkness; quit the night and seek the day.'

[7]

'Every real religion consists of <u>two parts</u>; the first part teaches what has to be done, this part becomes common knowledge, but in the course of time is distorted and departs from the original.

The second part teaches <u>how to do</u> what the first part teaches. This second part is preserved in secret in certain schools. With its help, it is always possible to rectify what has become distorted or to restore what has been forgotten!'

Quote from Gurdjieff: William Patrick Patterson

THE PRINCIPLE OF PAYMENT

On balance, it has to be said, that many New Age therapies and healing techniques are very valuable, however <u>some</u> are questionable to say the least. It is often fraudsters trying to cash in on the whole subject of New Age beliefs and also alternative medicines that give New Age activities a bad name. <u>It is very often undeserved</u> – a gentle alternative is on offer to that of damaging modern drugs.

Much is borrowed from Eastern religion and philosophy without understanding that these systems themselves are the fragmented remnants of a once glorious whole. Should we study Taoism or Buddhism for example, we will find that they are not complete systems of teachings; <u>there is so much missing</u> that they are, in reality, only partial systems of spiritual instruction. For example, Gurdjieff tells us that in the Buddhist religion of today <u>the inner core teachings of the Buddha have not reached the adherents of this path.</u> The reason he tells us this, is <u>because he knew exactly what the original teachings of Lord Buddha were</u>!

The Key to Religious and New Age Teachings

When we take sufficient time to study religious teachings of the world and also the various, so called, New Age teachings, we will find the most striking aspect of them all is not what they contain in terms of teachings but <u>what is missing in them</u>! For instance, 'The Eightfold Path of Buddhism' <u>is not the original teaching handed down by Lord Buddha to his closest disciples</u>!

Gurdjieff explained that each major religion has an outer teaching, which we see all around us in society today and, <u>an inner teaching</u>, which can no longer be found in secular society – it must be found through our own efforts! Only this inner teaching contains the practical methods for spiritual enfoldment: this critical practical teaching is missing <u>from all modern day religions and New Age teaching</u>.

Gurdjieff explained that all of the original transcendent teachings of the Earth had three component parts: a philosophical part, a theoretical part and a practical part! The philosophical and theoretical parts are sometimes transmitted via writings but the practical part is only transmitted orally – when the student has been prepared to receive such instruction. <u>It is never given to the unworthy</u>!

There is, of course, much Knowledge and high level principles missing in all of the aforementioned teachings, but let us take just one principle to begin with: the Principle of Payment. Gurdjieff stressed that it was necessary to pay for what one received on the Esoteric Path – otherwise there is no progress. It was not just money, his reference was also to sacrifice and diverse efforts made by the student.

Payment

The subject of payment is indeed a very important one – people will make great sacrifices and make high payments for material things but, when it comes to the spiritual world, these very same individuals are not willing to pay a single cent and believe that all should be free gratis.

Valuation

Payment is directly connected to the principle of valuation; if we value something then we will certainly pay for it. On the other hand, if we do not really value it, we will definitely not pay for it, and there are many ways of paying – effort, sacrifice, practice, attention, attendance, spiritual work, connecting the diverse elements of the teaching together, helping others through your own learning etc, etc.

'Question: Is the reason why this knowledge may not be given without payment, because people who take it without payment will twist it?'

'Answer: Simply because they will lose it, will throw it away, because valuation depends on payment. You cannot have a right valuation of a thing you do not pay for. If it comes too easily, you do not value it. This is one side, and another side of the question is that if you value a thing you will not give it away to other people.'

P.D. Ouspensky [8]

This idea of payment in return for what one receives on the Path, is critical, for if one is not prepared to make efforts, to sacrifice, to pay money for the time and efforts of others, then there is no question … we do not value it enough to pay!

'The idea of payment is very important and it must be understood that payment is absolutely necessary. One can pay in one way or another way and everyone has to find that out for himself. But nobody can get anything he does not pay for. Things cannot be given they can only be bought. It is magical, not simple. If one has knowledge, one cannot give it to another person, for only if he pays for it can the other person have it. This is a cosmic law.'

P.D. Ouspensky [9]

We find individuals who come to workshops and to group meetings and try to avoid paying, in one way or another. This only shows that they are unsuitable for esoteric work – <u>on a deep internal level, they do not value it</u>!

SHADOWS OF BRILLIANT WAYS

When we look around us and see all the diverse religions and New Age activities in society, we are actually viewing the 'shadows' of Great Ways, great esoteric teachings that once existed openly upon the Earth.

The great teachings for the inner-transformation-of-man have now become diluted or have disappeared altogether from ordinary life. There have been no esoteric schools, that is, no authentic schools, in Europe for 400 years according to Gurdjieff.

We see many spiritual lines, which no longer possess their 'inner-core', their inner or esoteric teachings. They have become divested of their power and their true significance – now only containing fragments of their former glory!

We see this with Buddhist, Christian, Hindu and other spiritual lines – as Gurdjieff tells us: the core of these teachings, as intended by their great founders, have not reached their modern day followers! This, despite the many adamant claims we hear from religious followers, once this fact is put to them – they simply object loudly and subsequently remain ignorant!

G. tells us however, that initiated wisdom still exists in certain physical locations, on the Earth; where a living wisdom tradition is perpetuated by an unbroken line of initiates. This is called 'the Chain of Transmission' by the Greater Sufi tradition.

He further tells us that the onus lies with us, where we are deeply interested in Truth and esoteric wisdom, to make contact or form a link to these, now hidden repositories of knowledge. We can bring this wisdom within our cognitive range!

This, he informs us, requires active work and effort on our part – it can never be achieved by hope or passive contemplation from our 'comfort zone'.

'Everyone is born into the world with one lesson to learn from the work standpoint, one task to perform in regard to himself, and unless he begins to see it, his life is really meaningless. You have to remember something we have all forgotten. Life is very short; we lose ourselves too early in life. Do not drift. Take hold of yourself and ask: "What am I doing? Where am I going?" Think what you must do before it is too late; think what is important for you to work on. Everyone has to distinguish in himself what has to be worked on, his reason for living his life. Man is born into this planet with an inner task and life is so arranged that he cannot find himself and his meaning through life alone, but only through seeing what this inner task is!'

Maurice Nicoll [10]

SIMPLE MINDS

In the sphere of 'esoteric writings' and 'groups', we find many 'teachers' and 'authoritative writers' putting forward theories on Gurdjieff, esotericism, the nature of Truth and much more besides. With a long-standing background in this subject and with the aid of <u>authentic teachers</u>, it is possible to separate the fakes, the novices, and the dilettantes, from those who are genuine and possess <u>real knowledge</u>.

It has to be said, few are those who are authentic in this field. Like an expert diamond merchant, it is possible to spot fakes very quickly and without hesitation - but only much experience gives this! Then an interesting phenomenon occurs...

With the expansion of our cognitive ability within the modalities of esoteric study, we not only gain a deeper insight into esoteric teachings but, we also begin to see in life/society, that which we did not perceive before. We begin to see through the lies, the half-truths, the facades and 'the accepted norms' for what they are! It is as if a veil is lifted from our eyes and we begin to see for the first time: much that was formerly blurred or hidden from our perception. We see for instance -

Many false ideas are injected into the minds of the young, through the medium of 'education'. Young people are taught to ignore the deeper questions about life, in favour of 'scientific questions', academia, narrow and banal logical thinking, thesis, sophistry and trite prepared answers. Many students are fearful of the college or university they attend, may react negatively to radical thinking or a radical thesis, and submit alternative work or work sanitised of those elements critical of the system. They fear 'being failed' by conservative exam boards or trite individual adjudicators. Thus, creativity and observed facets of our society are muted!

Now the young grow up with a battery of questions and answers, handed down by a false hierarchy of 'teachers' who themselves were handed a similar modus of study and thinking from their seniors. Thus we never escape the paradigm of logic and defective thinking. Most of all, we never question the very structure and modus operandi of the phoney system which instructs us so badly! We accept everything blindly – like so many sheep penned in by the farmer, ready for the now inevitable micro-management and exploitation: a subtle form of mind control!

The natural development of Essence-questioning is thus retarded and the young person grows up without ever having 'tasted' the exhilaration of genuine questions from Essence, manifesting naturally and spontaneously in their own consciousness! Through culture-bound-reasoning and the banal moulding of young minds, by a corrosive and inept 'education system', people now reach adulthood without any real knowledge about life. Many leave this 'education' without any development of the inner-qualities, principles, values and Being-abilities proper to an adult.

Today, young people leaving 'education' often lack incentive, basic qualities such as: communication skills, empathy with others, sincerity and humility. Many manifest the unbecoming qualities of selfishness and laziness, without any awareness that this behaviour should really be an embarrassment for them!

Wrong Education in Modern Man

'Through their influence, wise tutors can repair the psyche of those who have been mis-educated, if they watch over them for 2 years!'

Gurdjieff [11]

Thus, we find an 'education' system not fit for purpose, which produces young adults lacking many of the basic human qualities and virtues, which go to make up a balanced individual: capable of sustaining relationships with others and also leading a full, purposeful and fulfilling life. <u>These young adults later go on to be the professionals in our society: the doctors, lawyers, counsellors, estate agents, garage repair shop owners, bankers etc</u>.

One of the results of all of this is that society is breaking down and becoming more and more artificial. We see a rise in abnormal features in our societies; drug addiction, depression, lack of incentive for millions of people, low level mental illness in countless numbers of people, the loss of identity, banal consumerism, the rise of crime, family break-ups and inter-marital problems never witnessed before on such a scale. <u>People are lacking meaning in their lives</u>.

'Only through self-knowledge is knowledge of others practically possible. Only by seeing, knowing and understanding what is in you can you see, know and understand what is in another person. One of the greatest evils of human relationship is that people make no attempt to enter into one another's position but merely criticise one another without any restraint and do not possess any inner check to this mechanical criticism owing to the absence of any insight into themselves and their own glaring crudities, faults and shortcomings. As a result, not only do they not help each other, but the normal balance of things is upset, and by this I mean that an accumulation of wrong or evil psychic material is formed daily in human relationships and, in fact, in everyone's life, which should never exist if people saw themselves and others simultaneously, and in this way could neutralise the effect of their conduct day by day. This lack of psychological responsibility, both to oneself and to

others, is perhaps especially characteristic of modern times and is the source of one part of the widespread modern unhappiness that marks the present age, in which, amongst other things, there is a decline in even ordinary human kindness, with a resulting hardness which is among the most dangerous factors in regard to the future, and which effectually stops all possibility of the right development of the emotional life.'

Maurice Nicoll [12]

A FOUNDATION COURSE IN ESOTERIC WISDOM

This course is presented to the public to facilitate an approach to authentic esoteric materials and a wisdom from a bygone era; forgotten in the mists of time. The ability to recognise this wisdom is now mostly lost to modern man!

In the last century a powerful and dynamic spiritual teacher named G.I Gurdjieff brought *a core-teaching* to Europe; an esoteric teaching of a very high order! This teaching he said, came from pre-pharaonic Egypt; it was a teaching which had the power to transform, to create *new Being in a man or a woman!* Why pre-pharaonic Egypt?

Gurdjieff had spent almost 20 years in search of Truth and authentic Wisdom in the East, travelling through dangerous countries at the time, such as India, the Hindu Kush, Siberia, Turkmenistan, the Solomon Islands and Tibet. He intuited that the wisdom he sought could only be found through contact with a hidden and unbroken chain of initiated Knowledge, a wisdom from remote antiquity, which could now only be found in *wisdom schools or esoteric schools.* Finally, Gurdjieff had the breakthrough he sought and made contact with the *Sarmoung Brotherhood.* This brotherhood had survived since ancient times, from in fact, the early Babylonian period in history and was a repository of unequalled true esoteric wisdom and practice. He had found the fabled 'Great Temple': Jesus was said to have spent 12 years there, according to legend. (Here were also women in equal numbers according to Gurdjieff.)

Gurdjieff left this monastery a changed man; literally Gurdjieff was not the same person who entered the gates of this antique citadel. He was now an individual who had gone through incredible feats of spiritual endurance and training; he had reached his goal. Gurdjieff left the Sarmoung School with new powers and a high level of new consciousness; he would later use these powers to great effect in transmitting to others the wisdom he had acquired through great labour, for himself!

It is only when we have the courage to face things exactly as they are,
without any self-deception or illusion, that a light will develop out of events
by which the path to success may be recognised.

I-Ching [13]

Gurdjieff told his later followers, that the teaching he brought to Europe had its origins in pre-pharaonic Egypt. He said that the original teaching was in use during this time, when Egypt was green and the pharaonic dynasties of Egypt had as yet, not come into being. This ancient teaching of the transformation of man had survived *underground* through a succession of initiates and wisdom schools down through time.

Gurdjieff himself was set an obligation from the initiates who were his teachers, to bring this teaching to the West and spread it among the peoples of the Western World, during what was left of his physical life. Gurdjieff set about this task with great urgency and dynamism. With his newly developed powers and spiritual vision, he could see that Earth was now at a critical phase of its development. Man had created weapons of such magnitude; weapons, which could reach every part of the globe and even destroy the biosphere outright! Gurdjieff explained with characteristic candour '... *the Earth was not guaranteed survival; it was now placed on a "slippery slope" by man's own hubris and arrogance. Man's violent and warped temperament put into question the very survival of our planet. Not only this, but, man's unremitting exploitation of the Earth's natural resources, the removal of oil, gas, minerals and timber from the Earth's surface; was without a doubt, destabilising the integrity of Earth itself as an entity!'*

With this knowledge in hand, he set about preparing people in Europe and America, in the 1920s and 1930s, to receive initiated Knowledge and to transform as many people as possible; to create in his words *'as many people with natural Being as possible'*. He reasoned that only by changing mankind radically, could the Earth be saved from catastrophe and destruction in the future. Only by raising man's <u>level of Being</u> could this urgent task be achieved.

By raising man's level of Being, man's level of reason and responsibility for his own world could manifest for real.

Today, Gurdjieff's vision and acute sense of what is coming, has not yet been fully understood by society at large. Global warming is now the topic of the day, but was not even a presenting issue during Gurdjieff's time; he died in 1949.

Before he died, G. set his followers the task of spreading initiated Knowledge in society, to the best of their ability. This present volume pursues that aim!

To this end, there are groups all over the world today, teaching this wisdom which has emanated from this one man's vision. However, not all of these groups carry the original integrity nor initiated wisdom manifested by Gurdjieff himself. Some have been 'infected' by life's mundane corrosive and destructive effect on the psyche and integrity of man. Many have turned into cults and quasi-religious organisations. We do not endorse such organisations and cannot countenance any behaviour which puts integrity and high standards in jeopardy. Many do not truly understand the nature of initiated wisdom and seek only narrow self-interest; others to 'cash-in' on a trend, seeing things only from the outside as it were. However, there are a few individuals emerging from this mind-set who can see through the morass of fake groups and 'plastic leaders'. All is not lost!

The following esoteric materials have been arranged by Mr J. McKeaney: a long-time student of esotericism and teacher of Gurdjieff (and related materials). They represent a distillation of many years of active study and sincere exploration. It is only after breaking away from the bonds of logic; culture-bound reasoning and conditioning that we can truly begin to understand what is missing in that culture and develop a new cognitive ability outside of the race consciousness. We soon begin to perceive that, what is missing from our culture, is none other than the core elements needed for a harmonious and conscious life on planet Earth: and without which, felicity, social cohesion, understanding, mutual respect, and an objective approach to life, together with an enhanced cognitive level - can never manifest. Our true perception has been muted by the mechanical and artificial societal constructs around us: false emotional-anchors and pseudo-educational-modalities.

The value of these materials lie in the context that they are esoteric; coming to us from *higher mind* or, if you like, individuals spread over time, who have developed themselves and evolved to higher levels of consciousness and intelligence; having been aided in their quest by passing through wisdom schools/esoteric schools. Jesus Christ is a good example of this Paradigm!

One of the central tenets of esotericism is that, if an individual seeks truth, it is first of all necessary to throw off the conditioning and programming of ordinary life, before one can begin to understand or appreciate high-level teachings. This means that a special training or re-education is required; so that neural pathways in the seeker's brain are re-oriented and the filters implanted by mundane life – removed.

Without this special training, the filters possessed by the average person in ordinary life are too strong and, instead of deep pondering and contemplation resulting from contact with such materials and Knowledge, negative reactions are usually the order of the day. (Filters are greatly strengthened by 'education'.)

'What are the real connection between people? When the same Knowledge opens a doorway between them. When the same inner sight exists in you as in another, you are drawn to be companions.'

Rumi [14]

MISSION STATEMENT

The psyche of modern man is now such that, he no longer comprehends the nature of neither Initiated Wisdom nor the reason for his very existence here on Earth.

Gurdjieff has explained that his mission to disseminate authentic wisdom to the world was of critical importance, perhaps unparalleled in modern times. There are many tens of thousands of people around the world today seeking to understand the meaning of Gurdjieff's mission and the wisdom he brought to us.

'Man has become a blind and dangerous animal here on Earth; with too much power and no development of conscience.'

Gurdjieff [15]

Gurdjieff made gargantuan efforts to communicate the coming set of terrestrial problems to mankind. To this end he did not spare himself or his perceived reputation to those around him.

In this New Age of Aquarius, people are slowly beginning to wake up to the need for inner-work and authentic wisdom. To this end, there are a number of people today, who are 'an advanced guard', a nucleus of awareness manifesting here on Earth, who dare to show the Way. These people are now slowly beginning to show themselves, we can only wait and see how this will all play out over the coming years. We do not know if it will fail or succeed?

KNOWLEDGE

'Although we generally think that we understand what knowledge means, we do not understand that there are different levels of knowledge. We are, for instance, familiar with 'terrestrial knowledge' (knowledge with a small k), *we are not however, familiar with esoteric Knowledge or higher learning (Knowledge* with a capital K).

We do not even comprehend what higher Knowledge actually means? Because of a combination of elements in our now artificial society, such as our system of 'education', our present state of suggestibility and the loss of certain cognitive abilities – formerly possessed by us, high level Knowledge remains invisible to all but a fraction of terrestrials.

Man who lives entirely in personality (the mask or veneer), cannot employ his instrument, nor the cognitive functions proper to it, to perceive the existence of a Higher Learning on Earth: which exists on a much higher level than he!

[16]

INITIATED WISDOM

Gurdjieff explained that there are three definitive levels of Initiated Wisdom:

The first level is that of a general preparation in initiated wisdom; an opening of the person's mind to Truth and the concept of esoteric Knowledge. This level also involves removing false elements from the psyche of man and, then, working to develop new qualities and abilities necessary to perpetuate further development. This level is in many ways a preparation for the second level. (A man must challenge the lies which are implanted in him by society and its lack of conscience!)

- The second level is that of changing the inner-matrix of an individual, to a level where a new core understanding and inner stability is achieved. This involves a realignment of the seven chakras in a person to a new level: referred to in esotericism as *all centres balanced state*. At the end of this second level of initiation, an individual cannot return to their former level of ignorance … a new level of Being emerges. This level is, in real terms, a preparation for the third level.

- The third level of initiation is that of the Wisdom School. This represents the final level of True Initiation for a man or a woman. Both men and women are viewed equal under the auspices of The Great Way. With this level comes a preparation for prater human transformation: an emergent and new cosmic life form! (Cosmic Consciousness.)

'The strength of a man's position in the world depends on the degree of adequacy of his perception of reality. The less adequate it is, the more disoriented and hence insecure he is, and therefore the need of idols to lean on and thus find security.'
Erich Fromm [17]

INTERACTIVE WORKSHOPS

With our interactive workshops (not lectures) we provide the first level of initiation, for those individuals who seek it.

Workshops are structured to suit the psyche of contemporary peoples, with practical exercises and exploration of esoteric materials, to begin the process of change in the psyche and cognitive level of those who wish it.

These workshops are simple, yet unique and dynamic in ways that cannot be explained in the written word. Workshops are designed and structured to re-educate and open the neural-pathways in those attending. Also, these workshops are structured to begin the process of removing *filters* implanted by mundane life and pseudo-social-structuring. To this end we examine the subject of 'false emotional-anchors' and the negative effect these have on the average individual. Often the direct recognition of the power of a false emotional-anchor, will remove its harmful manifestation in a person's life!

We work on *a deep structure level* and begin the process of moving away from *surface structure* cognition and learning. This is a training which some will fail and others will use wisely. Nothing is guaranteed, but an opening in perception is possible, which cannot be generated in ordinary life conditions.

We invite all who are genuinely interested to apply to attend these unique and highly motivational courses. Many people experience an expansion of awareness and other dormant faculties. It is, of course, designed to act as a catalyst, to steer people towards a new understanding of themselves, their potentialities and a new vision of the Cosmos which surrounds them.

On certain occasions, participants have been known to spontaneously shift consciousness into the third level or self-remembering – a level of Being called the 'Witnessing Consciousness' by the Buddhists. This event is sometimes triggered by work and new cognitive functions opening within individuals in the group.

Such an event creates great excitement and awe within the group: as the other participants can sense the emergent energy-shift within the person concerned.

It should be noted that these shifts of consciousness are often spontaneous and are not planned within the regime of the group work. However, these leaps of cognitive level (should they occur) are helpful for the student to verify the actual existence of these higher states of consciousness in the first place.

During the workshops we begin the exploration of materials brought directly by Gurdjieff himself and others written by his students during their time spent with him. The exploration of these materials forms the core of each period or workshop, giving practical examples and psycho-spiritual exercises to be experimented with, between sessions. Results are then surveyed during the subsequent meeting.

Students are taught to *core* all materials thus explored and also, not to accept anything at face value but to <u>verify all in personal experience and pondering</u>!

Students are also taught how to move away from conventional models of learning and how to adopt a new praxis for <u>real learning</u> and authentic Knowledge. Students will learn to differentiate between the different levels of terrestrial learning and authentic Higher Learning.

Many auxiliary materials will be used from Buddhist, Taoist, Sufi and Hindu traditions. These often add colour and grace to a subject already pregnant with potential and insight.

On occasions, spontaneous elements are introduced into the teaching models when it is deemed that students are ready. This can mean new practical exercises, trips outside the normal workshop area or, spontaneous chi-gung sessions to change the energy of the group.

'Just one great idea can completely change your life!'

Earl Nightingale [18]

'As you have heard, Gurdjieff said his task, in trying to teach Western people the Work – to quote his actual words – lay in "quarrelling ruthlessly with all manifestations dictated in people by the evil factor of vanity present in their Being." Gurdjieff said also: "We should be god-like creatures capable of entering into and understanding the position of others – of understanding the psyche of our neighbour".
But, he added, in so many words, "this is impossible because of the factor of vanity, which, admiring only itself, feels itself better than others and so produces not only wrong impressions but wrong results outwardly; which cause wrong connections internally, preventing any deepening of man or woman."'

Maurice Nicoll [19]

SUBJECTS COVERED IN THE WORKSHOPS WILL INCLUDE:

- Essence and Personality
- The Four Ways
- The Principle of Knowledge and Being
- The Law of Deviation of Forces
- The Law of Accident and Other Great Terrestrial Laws
- Man as a Sleeping Entity
- False Schools
- The Idea of Developing New Cognitive Abilities
- Understanding versus 'Head Knowledge or Academia'
- Internal and External Considering
- Negative Emotions and their Gradual Elimination
- The Principle of Transformation of man
- Active and Passive Suffering
- The Three Sacred Impulses for Man
- The Principle of Sacrifice
- The Ray of Creation and its Practical Application for Us
- The Four States of Consciousness
- Alchemy and the Three Photo-Plasmic Bodies
- Esoteric Schools
- The Masters of Wisdom
- Bridging
- Identification
- Objective and Subjective Art
- The Three Levels of Karma
- The Fall of Man
- Solar and Lunar Currents in Society
- Filters in Man's Psyche
- Man's Loss of Cognitive Abilities Over the Past Five Millennia
- The Four Levels of Thinking
- A New and Definitive Approach to the Seven Chakra System
- The Enneagram

FILTERS IN MAN'S PSYCHE

A critical element in all of this, are the filters implanted in man's psyche through the hypnotism of mundane life and the emergent maladjusted structure of modern society. The filters present in the psyche of modern man, prevent him from perceiving Truth. He is unaware of his own inner psychology and its definitive dwindling in sophistication over the past five millennia. And so it is, that man today, stands completely unaware of his predicament, a situation which shows no sign of improvement. (Gurdjieff called these 'filters' in his teaching - 'buffers'.)

Neither does modern man know anything about his potentialities or the efforts required by Great Nature, for him to manifest those supernormal potentialities. Mankind has lost a number of original cognitive powers!

The situation has now arisen, that should an individual decide to seek Truth, it is first necessary to receive a special preparation, in order to facilitate this end. It is no longer possible for a man to perceive Truth just by merely wishing it; a man must develop a whole new range of understanding, qualities and abilities in himself before this can begin to happen. A transition period must now elapse, and crucial to this process, the individual's chakra system is opened in a particular manner; a person is prepared to receive Truth! (New cognitive abilities are developed.)

What does this mean in real terms? It means, that should one present real and authentic Knowledge and Wisdom to any person you care to mention in life; even where they are 'seeking this Knowledge', they will neither understand nor recognise it! They will pass over it and think you a complete fool, with very few exceptions. And, even where, by chance, a person acknowledges the veracity of this wisdom … tomorrow it is all forgotten! People are so powerfully attached to false emotional-anchors and pseudo-societal-structures, such as our modern 'education' system and 'scientific discoveries', the lure of possessions and a consumer mentality, that no space is vacant in their emotional-field for Knowledge of a higher order.

'Knowledge is generally confused with information. Because people are looking for information or experience, they do not find Knowledge. You cannot avoid giving Knowledge to one fitted to receive it. You cannot give Knowledge to the unfit, this is impossible. You can, if you have it and, if the person is capable, fit a person for receiving Knowledge.'

Sayed Najmuddin [20]

Such is the strength of *the hypnotism of ordinary life* - because of this strange predicament in the psyche of modern man, a person now values those elements from life which are unimportant and, neglects those elements which could give him *something real.*

Because man now lives below his legitimate level of Being, he has forfeited his real and genuine possibilities in relation to the development of his spiritual life!

Today, mankind <u>cannot receive high level Knowledge without a special period of preparation first</u>! Included in this work is the removal of false emotional-anchors.

'Be aware, that the science which provides the bridge between the inner and outer life of an individual, is rare, and is transmitted only to those who have been prepared beforehand. It always happens, that there will be many who will prefer to accept imitation in place of reality; the superficial in place of true wisdom!'

Hadrat Muinudin Chisti: Founder of The Chisti Sufi Order [21]

'Some people say they haven't found themselves. The self is not something one finds; it is something one creates.'

Thomas Szasz [22]

False Emotional-Anchors

Societal influences create many false and deviant emotional-anchors in us: our modern 'education' is one of the principle modes through which this happens, and is itself a very powerful false emotional-anchor!

What are False Emotional-Anchors?

False emotional-anchors are interests, attitudes and behaviour patterns we adopt from our surroundings and since our culture is totally artificial; a totally artificial construct with nothing real in it, no substance, our emotional-anchors are not real either. Our entire emotional-field as an individual becomes superficial and deviant. <u>We become jaded superficial people</u>!

So we have many pseudo interests, habits and fads such as football, gambling, shopping and the consumer ethos, fashion, the news bulletin, cinema, the latest gadget, television, sexism, racism, ageism, prescription drugs in certain countries such as the U.S.A., recreational drug use, smoking, alcohol, dangerous sexual practices, computer games, computer addiction – the list goes on. It is also interesting to note that some of these activities cause low-level mental illness in great numbers of people! It could be said that one of the characteristics of today's society is this low-level mental illness which often sits just below the level of our 'cognitive-radar'.

The two most dangerous false emotional-anchors in today's society are: our modern 'education' and the rarely questioned: pharmaceutical medicine!

To explain in a direct and concise way, just how a person is connected to these emotional-anchors, I will use the example of 'education' itself.

'Education is a form of imposed ignorance'

Noam Chomsky [23]

People in general place great stores of emotional capital in very many of the societal elements just mentioned – including that of 'education'. Should you criticise or question in an informed fashion this famous 'education', you may find that people respond in a most unexpected way. Far from pondering the veracity of your comments and observations, most people will respond in a violent and aggressive fashion, as if you had just made a personal attack upon them, themselves. The reason for this is that, modern 'education' is just another emotional-anchor that people invest a lot of emotional capital in: they identify with modern 'education' heavily, see it as part of their personal identity and cannot separate themselves from it psychologically and emotionally. So, when this famous 'education' is called into question or examined forensically, which by the way, modern people never do, they respond as if you had made a personal attack on them or a close family member. Gurdjieff calls this attachment 'Identification'.

In fact, what really happens is a negative reaction and not an intelligent, measured and coherent response. That is because people 'carry with them' artificial and, of course, prepared answers, at all times. ('Education' generates prepared answers – answers which are trite, stale, imitative and borrowed!)

'They wanted to protect you, they wanted you to be ready to face any crisis in your life, so they supplied you answers – and answers cannot be supplied: answers have to be found … one has to pay for answers. They are not cheap. Knowledgeability is not Knowledge!'

Osho [24]

In fact, man's conditioning is so complete and all pervasive, that the vast majority of people reading the above will neither understand nor agree with it in general.

Modern 'Education'

The problem facing modern people with regard to what they call 'education' is very complex and will require some amount of exploration here.

Although modern education purports to bring out the best in each individual according to their abilities, this is far from true and indeed, in centuries to come, people may well laugh and raise their eyebrows in wonderment at our ineptitude and naivety. Modern 'education' produces automatons <u>without real cognitive abilities and the crucial qualities and abilities which every Being should have</u>!

For a human being to develop harmoniously, it is necessary that all three parts of their Being are instructed together. The intellectual centre, the emotional centre and the moving/instinctive centre must all function in harmony with one another: it is particularly critical, that mind and emotions should work together in full and complete synergy as <u>this produces a new cognitive-force in the individual</u>.

In modern 'education', the intellectual centre (or mind) is the main focus of all instruction, without due consideration of the emotional life (Essence) of the individual or indeed the physical/instinctive life of that person. Also, all <u>true education</u> is individually tailored around the student; traits, talents and qualities particular to that person must always be borne in mind, not *a one size fits all approach* as is the case with today's teaching modalities. <u>Personality thus grows disproportionately</u> in the individual, creating major imbalances and a narrow world view. <u>The mind and cognitive range of the student is thus cynically moulded</u>!

Without this training of the emotional centre, <u>the critical 'building blocks' of a person's character and qualities are completely neglected</u>! As a result of this, all major qualities of the individual reside in Personality and not in Essence.

And, to translate – this simply means that the individual's qualities remain superficial … these types of influences do not filter through to Essence!

Education is seen as a means of obtaining a better position in life or acquiring wealth, not as a tool for enlarging the person themselves on an internal level. And so, <u>all education today is external, so to speak</u>! The person's inner life, which is by far the more important, is left to its own devices. There is also a very real and covert sub-text to conform to the prevailing paradigm of the day, in our education. Tuition is loaded with numerous false emotional-anchors, which prevail in the very modus operandi of that particular culture; at that particular time.

The net result of all of this, is that people focus on that which is unreal and vacuous and fail to value and act upon those elements in their lives which are real – those elements which could bring something dynamic, something of substance; new enhanced cognitive abilities … a new perception of the real purpose of their life!

THE 'EDUCATED FOOL'

Today, we have an entirely new phenomenon at large – 'the educated-fool'!
The individual who has much 'education' but very little ability or being-quality: people who 'know much' but can do little. Unfortunately, this type being a product of 'the system'- is highly suggestible and cannot discern <u>what is missing</u> in his or her learning; nor the fact that <u>their cognitive range</u> is not at all what it should be! (In the beginning, cognitive range is everything!)

It is through the current vacuous 'education system' that this situation has come into being. They form, what was termed <u>the mechanogencia</u> in ancient times and cannot perceive the true nature of the maladjusted society they live in! And it is mostly these types who later become societies' leaders, e.g. politicians, doctors, lawyers, 'professionals' etc. Thus, the cycle of crass ineptitude is perpetuated and we see very little change in our contemporary society as a result! People remain <u>highly suggestible</u> and <u>easily influenced</u> by the now many false societal constructs and banal cultural activities: now everywhere accepted as <u>real culture</u>! Without Essence development, people remain devoid of all <u>real</u> cognitive abilities! <u>The student is not allowed to develop a deep critical faculty - think for themselves</u>!

> *'However much you study,*
> *You cannot know without action.*
> *A donkey laden with books is neither*
> *A wise man nor an intellectual.*
> *Empty of essence, what learning has he –*
> *whether upon him is firewood or books?'*

Saadi of Shiraz [25]

'The average man today thinks very little for himself. He remembers data as presented by the schools and the mass media; he knows practically nothing of what he knows by his own observing and thinking. Nor does his use of things require much thought or skill. One type of gadget requires no skill or effort at all, as for instance the telephone. Another type of gadget, the automobile, requires some initial learning and after a while, when it has become routine, only a very small amount of personal effort or skill is required. Nor does modern man – including the educated groups – think much about religious, philosophical, or even political problems. He ordinarily adopts one or the other of the many clichés offered him by political and religious books or speakers, but the conclusions are not arrived at by active and

penetrating thinking of his own. He chooses the cliché that appeals most to his own character and social class.'

Erich Fromm [26]

Now Gurdjieff tells us that because of the dwindling of the psyche of Man and the subsequent results obtaining from this, the psyche of people gradually began to be divided into two distinct states; a 'two system-Zoostat' – what is now commonly referred to today, as man's conscious and subconscious minds. He tells us that this state is not natural for terrestrials but began to form in us just after the destruction of the continent Atlantis.

'... the functioning of their 'being-consciousness', began to be divided in two
and when two entirely different consciousnesses having nothing in common with each other were gradually formed in them, namely, those two different consciousnesses, the first of which was called by them simply 'consciousness' and the second – when they finally noticed it in themselves – was called and still continues to be called 'subconsciousness'.

Gurdjieff [27]

It should be noted here, that Man's subconscious mind and his Essence are uniquely connected. Essence represents what is man's own – Personality a mere fake veneer! What is contained in this subconscious mind is real and valuable; by contrast, man's conscious mind is a mere artificial cultural construct! (Our subconscious mind is not Essence - but is directly related!)

'Only thanks to this single fact that your favourites, especially the contemporary ones, do not know at all or even suspect the necessity of at least adapting their famous education to the said subconscious of their offspring, but that they always and in everything intentionally assist every one of the rising generation to perceive impressions only from the abnormally artificial, then thanks only to this, when every one of them reaches the age of responsible being, all his being-judgements and all his deductions from them are always purely peculiarly-subjective to him and have no connection with not only genuine being-impulses arising also in him ....'

Gurdjieff [28]

And so a type of subtle programming occurs in the individual from a very early age. False emotional-anchors or values and cognitive modalities are implanted in young people via 'education' and this programming will determine the individual's vision and world-view thereafter; arresting the development of real intelligence, insight and objective essence - questioning, in later life.

'Thanks only to such a, in the objective sense, maleficence, but according to their naïve subjective understanding 'benevolence' towards their offspring, all the sacred data put in by Great Nature Herself for forming in them their real being-consciousness become isolated and remain during the entire period of their existence in their almost primitive state...'

Gurdjieff [29]

In other words, all of the objective data necessary for the full and harmonious development of the individual is found in his subconscious-mind/Essence! Essence development in Man is thus retarded. Personality or 'the mask' carried by a man is strengthened, and what one might call <u>the pseudo-man emerges</u>.

'For your wider understanding of this particular 'psychic state' it is necessary to tell you further that even up to now they arise with every kind of data for acquiring genuine being-reason, and at their arising ... there is not yet in their presences ... the said '<u>false-consciousness</u>'. But only later, during their development and their preparation to become responsible beings, either by themselves or by the intentional directing of their as they call them 'parents' or 'teachers' – that is to say, responsible beings who undertake the responsibility of the preparation of the given beings for responsible existence – they begin, as I said, to help intentionally in taking in and fixing those impressions which later are data for the impulses corresponding to surrounding abnormally established conditions; and only then, being gradually formed, there just begins to be in their common presence this said <u>artificially formed 'consciousness'</u> of theirs.'

Gurdjieff [30]

Let us take another example of false emotional-anchors: the consumer ethos in society. Should we examine sincerely and with genuine candour our shopping habits and possessions, we will surely come to the astute conclusion that we have no real need for perhaps as much as 50% of what we own. In other words, shopping and purchasing luxury goods gives us a type of 'emotional-fix'; a feeling of power and mobility in society – all of which is a great illusion.

'The basis for any approach to self-transformation is an ever-increasing awareness of reality and the shedding of illusions.'

Erich Fromm [31]

Yet another false emotional-anchor, is that of how <u>we think</u>, we are completely free, partly because of modern technology and also, of course, societal suggestion. <u>Our conditioning is all pervasive and complete</u>!

'Yet precisely because of the gigantic power and size of the bureaucracy of the state, army, industry, the replacement of personal bosses with impersonal bureaucracies, the individual became more powerless than he was, even before – but he is not aware of his powerlessness.

In order to defend himself against such an individually and socially disturbing awareness, he has now built up an ideal of absolute, unrestricted "personal" freedom.'

Erich Fromm [32]

LAWS GOVERNING MAN'S EXISTENCE ON EARTH

Here we will look at three laws which Gurdjieff tells us affect our ordinary life at all times, and without our awareness. In volume two, we will look at the gradual decline of human civilizations, and other intriguing esoteric materials.

The Law of Accident:

Ouspensky describes this as 'when an event happens without any connection with the line of events we observe, if one accident does not happen – another will.'

The Law of Accident refers to Personality and the False-Ego; when Essence starts to develop strongly in us we are less under this law and come under a higher law, the Law of Fate! For the present we will mainly consider these two primary laws.

People in general, ordinary people, live almost entirely under the law of accident. It simply means that most of the events in our lives, including the major 'important ones', are, in reality, viewed from the wider circle of events, purely accidental. Another way of looking at this is that the activities in our life have no substance! The meaning we attribute to our activities is purely subjective and programmed into us by larger societal forces outside of our control and awareness.

From our conditioned cognitive level we find it very difficult to understand the Law of Accident. However, it is possible to see its effects in people around us, rather than in ourselves – to begin with. Our vanity often blinds us to its existence.

The Law of Fate

Fate means we come under planetary laws – we are beginning to develop into 'natural Beings' with enhanced cognitive awareness and qualities proper to a planetary Being. Fate means we begin to live in Essence – to shed 'the herd-mentality' and live a more natural life, not absorbed in external fake cultural activities. We begin to move away from the artificial elements in life and 'wake up'!

In order to clarify these laws somewhat, it is necessary here to use examples. If we take the man who sits on the corner and drinks beer from a can for extended periods of time, does not work or engage in activities necessary for normal day-to-day existence – we find a person who is considerably under the Law of Accident.

The vast majority of things which happen to him in his life are accidents: from the local priest accidently being in the neighbourhood and taking pity on him and offering help, to getting hit by a bus the following week as he crosses the road in a state of drunkenness and subsequently going to hospital with a broken leg!

We find, if we examine his life very closely, that it is a complete disaster; we find a life full of strife, accidents, suffering, delusions, wrong thinking and futile pursuits. If we look very carefully we will find this Law of Accident at 'every turn'.

Now, if we take the monk in the monastery; the life he or she leads – it is a life of directed harmony and peace ... strife and accident scarcely exist there. The life of the monk is balanced and coordinated, the monk comes under the Law of Fate! In such a life and environment, everything is geared towards understanding, mutual co-operation, felicity, compassion and kindness to one another. One is instantly under higher cosmic laws! Essence then becomes the active force in the monk!

The above example shows two different individuals, living on one planet but under two different cosmic laws. The difference is in the quality of one's life ... the inner-quality. Personality reflects planetary influences and therefore is subject to many more laws and inferior influences! When we render Personality passive and our Essence becomes active, we immediately place ourselves under the Law of Fate and thus, under fewer cosmic laws. Remember, the Law of Accident places us under 96 orders of laws, whereas the Law of Fate places us under only 24 orders of laws. (See diagrams at the end of Volume 1 for more on Essence and Personality.)

'Moreover, it happens fairly often that essence dies in a man while his personality and his body are still alive. A considerable percentage of people we meet in the streets of a great town are people who are empty inside, that is, they are actually already dead.

It is fortunate for us that we do not see and do not know it. If we knew what a number of people are already dead and what a number of these dead people govern our lives, we should go mad with horror.'

P.D. Ouspensky [33]

The Law of Will

This law refers to an intensive training of the individual in high-level esoteric work - it is always connected to altering the functioning of the energy centres or chakras in the student. It is serious work and has a definitive aim, whilst working under the supervision of those who have superior esoteric knowledge and the wisdom to implement specific changes within that individual.

This work under the will of another is key, since it is no ordinary spiritual work; such as Bakti Yoga or Raja Yoga - it is a modality that cannot be found existing openly in ordinary society.

Diagram of Cosmic Laws:

FALSE-EGO	96 ORDERS OF LAWS	MOON	LAW OF ACCIDENT	SUFFERING
PERSONALITY	48 ORDERS OF LAWS	EARTH	LAW OF ACCIDENT	MECHANICAL LIFE
ESSENCE	24 ORDERS OF LAWS	PLANETS	FATE	NEW AWARENESS
REAL 'I'	12 ORDERS OF LAWS	SUN	LAW OF WILL	THIRD LEVEL OF CONSCIOUSNESS

THE DIMINISHING OF MAN'S COGNITIVE ABILITIES

('THE FALL OF MAN')

Man's natural cognitive status is to be fully aware of his position in the Cosmos and the fact that he <u>needs to complete himself</u> – he is not completed by nature!

Gurdjieff tells us in his magnum opus, *Beelzebub's Tales* to his Grandson, that our cognitive abilities have, in very real terms, diminished since the early Babylonian times – two and a half thousand years BC - a process which began just after the destruction of Atlantis.

Gurdjieff explains that there are several cognitive elements missing in modern man's psyche, which were formerly his:

The first cognitive ability missing in modern man is that which we now refer to as our 'subconscious mind'; should manifest in our conscious mind, or if you like - should participate in our conscious mind. This division in the psyche of man was unknown back then – it is only in modern man that this strange anomaly has appeared. Even 4,500 years ago, man's psyche far exceeded our present status.

G. mentioned that the sacred data implanted there – namely: 'faith', 'hope', 'love' and 'conscience', no longer manifest in our ordinary consciousness, as was first ordained by the cosmic intelligences around us. This phenomenon came about chiefly because of the reduction of man's life principle, from Foolasnitamnian to Itoclanoz and also, from the surrounding abnormal conditions of external life!

The participation of the above functions in the psyche of man, alters his cognitive ability, fundamentally. A man becomes 'a higher type of Being' immediately.

The second cognitive ability missing in modern man is his ability to recognise and understand that he is not complete and that there is <u>something very significant missing in him</u>.

The third cognitive element absent in him is the perception to see, sense and also understand that knowledge exists on different levels and that terrestrial science and knowledge is not the highest in our world! There is something more! (A wisdom just outside modern Man's cognitive range!)

The fourth cognitive ability lost to man is that of retention of higher Knowledge, newly perceived. Gurdjieff tells us that today, people no longer have the capacity to retain High Level Knowledge: 'what is perceived or witnessed today is very often forgotten tomorrow'. This was not the case in ancient times according to G.

The cognitive ability required to approach esoteric teachings is quite high – it is, in fact, above average. However, cognitive ability can be greatly increased by the active study of authentic esoteric materials – that is, by engaging our emotional functions as we study and not just an intellectual or academic approach. We thus generate a new force in ourselves, when we engage our emotions while studying.

Further, man has now become highly suggestible and is easily influenced by the vacuous and shallow elements in his surroundings. He has ceased to think for himself but relies on the opinions of others, fashionable theories, television, the 'herd-mentality' and a pseudo-education. Then he pretends he knows – this is where lying manifests in its most powerful form! In fact – he knows nothing!

The fifth cognitive ability missing in modern man is his failure to think for himself.

It is difficult for an individual to break free from the false mental and emotional constructs of society – after all, he has many emotional anchors and vested interests in the society; and 'powerful people' now recognise his 'achievements'.

He never questions the ethos or structure of his surroundings and trite artificial societal mind-sets. He now accepts everything without question or pondering. Deep in Man's being is the desire for revolutionary change, but his surface mind or consciousness is timid, lazy, vacuous and highly suggestible! He is now, more than ever before, easily hypnotised by the 'glitter' and 'attractions' of external life!

'If a man becomes too polished by modern education, it becomes impossible for him to approach Truth or esoteric teachings.'

Gurdjieff [34]

'The new does not arise out of you it comes from the beyond. It is not part of you. Your whole past is at stake. The new is discontinuous with you, hence the fear. You have lived in one way, you have thought in one way, you have made a comfortable life out of your beliefs. Then something new knocks on the door... Everybody in the world wants to become new; because nobody is satisfied with the old. Nobody can ever be satisfied with the old because whatever

it is you have known it. Once known it has become repetitive, once known it has become boring, monotonous. You want to get rid of it. You want to explore, you want an adventure. You want to become new, and yet when the new knocks on the door, you shrink back, you withdraw, you hide in the old. This is the dilemma.'

Osho [35]

PERSONALITY CANNOT RETAIN ESOTERIC KNOWLEDGE

The first thing to be understood is that personality cannot fully comprehend high level authentic esoteric Knowledge <u>nor can it retain it for very long</u>!

It is really only Essence which comprehends and retains high level esoteric Knowledge: that is, <u>evolved Essence</u>, only developed Essence has the cognitive ability to do this. Personality at best can only <u>try to memorise</u> esoteric wisdom!

So, here we learn why esoteric wisdom is not popular with everyone and why only a small number of people can approach and absorb high level wisdom –

Personality is anchored in logic and defective thinking, and has little or no ability to think psychologically (emotional intelligence). <u>Personality is very limited</u>!

The Four Levels of Thinking

- Defective Thinking
- Logical Thinking
- Psychological Thinking or Emotional Intelligence (function of Essence)
- Esoteric Thought

Defective Thinking

With defective thinking we see an individual with numerous wrong attitudes to almost everything – defective thinking comes from wrong attitudes in us! The phenomenon of this type of mental level is always connected with the person being unable to see certain obvious realities – of course, not obvious to him or her. It represents a cognitive level below that of logic.

We see many examples of defective thinking in history: the flat Earth theory, the idea that the sun revolved around the Earth and, drilling holes in a person's skull to release evil spirits – a practice from medieval medicine.

Logical Thinking

Logical thinking is what people use most of the time, it is used to calculate, to read maps, to check our bank statements, to plan a holiday, in our speech, in our writing and use of computers, in a thousand and one things. However, logical thinking is *linear* and very limited in nature. Logic always involves the use of only one chakra; one centre in us, the mind or intellectual centre.

However, logic cannot properly understand or retain esoteric Knowledge: it is simply not sophisticated enough a modality for this purpose. Logic is the standard cognitive mode of modern man, together with defective thinking, both of which connect personality to the outer world.

A good example of logic in modern man, is that of his idea, that <u>all levels</u> of knowledge can be approached and understood by the mind – it being only a matter of the time spent studying same. This, of course, is very far from the truth and we can see just how erroneous this view is, when we ourselves develop the ability to think psychologically and make new and exciting cognitive discoveries concerning our own inner-world potentialities, and the vast chasm existing between ordinary terrestrial knowledge and high level esoteric Knowledge.

We quickly find our logical friends unable to comprehend our words and vision relating to higher learning – <u>we have left them behind</u>. Their logic becomes their limit! We formerly looked upon them as intelligent; now we see things somewhat differently – we have come to understand that different levels of intelligence exist even among ordinary people; the academic world exposes its stark limitations.

Psychological Thinking

Psychological thinking implies the wedding together of mind and emotions, in our cognitive instrument. Gurdjieff tells us that with the development of emotional intelligence, <u>a new force is formed in us</u>! Psychological thinking gives us the ability to understand and retain arcane Knowledge and use it in our daily lives: it allows us to <u>connect diverse high level ideas and principles into a cohesive whole</u>. This connective paradigm is what is valuable; with logic we are unable to see the connections between things in the esoteric world, whereas with the use of psychological thinking we enter a 'new paradigm' of interconnectedness and reciprocity. This type of thinking implies the use of at least three centres in us!

A good example of this thinking is when we experience major breakthroughs of deep insight and understanding – often in the active study of esotericism itself!

Esoteric Thought

This level of cognition is in fact not a mode of thought as we understand it. It is rather a state of consciousness. In this modality, cognition is direct, with no thoughts interceding between you and that which is perceived! This is called Self-Remembering by Gurdjieff and, called the Witnessing Consciousness by Buddhists. It is sometimes referred to as 'the Kiss of Ra' by esoteric writers and those who have experienced its magic.

YOUR LEVEL OF BEING ATTRACTS YOUR LIFE

In reality, regardless of what we see written in modern books etc, regarding 'the law of attraction' – <u>our Being attracts our life</u>! In other words, who you are intrinsically attracts your life!

It is mere 'child's play' to demonstrate this, for those who have the requisite cognitive level. <u>Remember, intellectual ability does not equate to cognitive level</u>.

The majority of people we find in society live between Personality and the False-Ego, usually a combination of both. People move into Essence only rarely!

Summary:

False-Ego ....under 96 order of laws
Personality...under 48 orders of laws
Essenceunder ....24 orders of laws
Real 'I' (Witnessing consciousness) .... under 12 orders of laws

The higher our Being development, the fewer laws govern us, by contrast, and for example – if we live say entirely in the False-Ego, the more laws we find ourselves under; the less free we are, and thus, the more we suffer!

So, from the above we can clearly see, the higher we reach in terms of our Being-development, the freer we are and subsequently we attract different events, people, careers, situations, karma etc, into our lives!

For instance, a person living almost entirely in the False-Ego is quite literally suffering for much of their 'conscious' existence and also causing others to suffer greatly too! (They are firmly under the Law of Accident.) Their life moves continuously from crisis to crisis! It is a kind of 'living nightmare' and they attract the wrong situations, people, events, influences and partners into their lives!

For the individual living between the False-Ego and Personality, their life is a very mechanical and repetitive one; with much boredom, jealousy, crude resentment, unfulfilled desires, unnecessary conflict, useless strife, etc.

On the other hand, a person living in Essence, lives a much simpler life, out of 'the limelight'; avoiding the 'participation mystique' and the 'consumer-culture'. There is often a noticeable lessening of conflict and crisis in this person's life. However, this does not mean a lack of effort or somehow this person 'just sails comfortably through life'; living in Essence means coming under planetary laws and this indicates a person 'in touch with their destiny', an individual aware of what direction they are going – then, life becomes a whole new challenge.

Living in Essence

So, we see that there are no less challenges, effort and struggle in a person's life, but there is clarity, a simplicity and integrity that is missing from Personality! This is so, because Essence feeds on Truth.

Essence is under 24 orders of laws, there is candour instead of duplicity, honesty in place of lies, insight into life, sensitivity and compassion; where Essence is correctly developed. There is also, for the first time, the appearance of integrity: especially when Essence is informed by true wisdom!

Real 'I' or the Witnessing Consciousness

This is the third state of consciousness possible for Man, it is under 12 orders of laws. In this state of super-cognition we begin to 'witness' life impartially for the first time or, at least, we achieve the first level of 'cosmic impartiality'.

We no longer experience fear, hate and anger as before; these emotions now manifest as 'ripples on the pond of life', they come and go very quickly – without the same 'flavour' or intensity. This is the 'bubble of silence' mentioned in the next section – one which places the individual in a totally new relationship to life! Real 'I' is the aim of all esoteric work – via the twin modalities of working on both Knowledge and Being. This is the true meaning of the fabled Shangri-la!

In this state of consciousness, we will attract a totally different life, than say, a person living in the False-Ego or Personality. The difference will be profound – all false-friends, pursuits, interests, situations will tend to 'fall away' from the individual's 'life-stream'. Lies from others become transparent and those around you will notice you have changed; you have become more silent and composed.

It is interesting to note here, that modern people have never even heard of this third state of consciousness possible for Man. Neither do they comprehend the concept of Being-development and all of the ramifications connected to this!

In fact, modern people have no concept of how important it is that one should have a profound focus on Being; which always begins with the development of good qualities in the individual.

These good qualities, such as courage, sincerity, humility, integrity, tenacity etc, form the 'bedrock' of any future development of Being in a person. There can be no imitation – either a person has these good qualities or they don't: but it often happens that <u>people try to disguise this lack of development</u>, but in reality, fail.

THE FOUR LEVELS OF CONSCIOUSNESS

There are four states of consciousness possible for terrestrial Beings. This has been established by ancient esoteric science and perhaps even more importantly by those who have attained to authentic higher levels of Being.

The primary two levels are accessible to us in our ordinary consciousness of everyday life, but the second two levels are not accessible to us during our ordinary state, without special measures or steps. The primary two levels we call 'unconscious' and 'waking-consciousness'. The unconscious state is when we are asleep and all of the chakras are disconnected from each other. Waking-consciousness on the other hand is our everyday state, sometimes referred to in esoteric teachings as the <u>robotic-level</u>.

It is necessary to transcend these first two basic levels of consciousness in order to progress spiritually. This means <u>not just entering</u> higher levels of Being which are possible for us but <u>fixing them and making them permanent in us</u>!

The two higher levels of consciousness which are possible for us are called the 'Witnessing Consciousness' and 'Objective Consciousness' respectively. The state of Witnessing Consciousness is our natural birthright to begin with; however <u>we have fallen</u> and today we no-longer achieve this state as a matter of course. We now have to acquire it <u>by our own efforts</u>. Within the level of Objective Consciousness, there is a higher 'core' possible, called Cosmic Consciousness; however, it is considered to be within the parameters of the fourth state.

From this we can see that we actually operate below the cognitive level we were created to achieve during our existence – below our natural status and birthright. We actually live in a state below that which Great Nature intended for us.

'The Bubble of Silence'
The experience of the third state of consciousness or Witnessing Consciousness is accompanied by *the bubble of silence* phenomenon. In this state, a bubble of silence descends upon us and we enter a new cognitive mode; those around us appear distant and unreal, we feel we are <u>witnessing life</u> for the first time – and of course, this is true.

This third state of consciousness is the aim of all schools, all religions and all spiritual work: in all epochs. It is the core element sought in esoteric work: all higher learning, all spiritual exercises and all understanding we seek to develop in ourselves are geared ultimately, towards *distilling from life* this vital inner-state!

THE THREE SACRED IMPULSES FOR MAN

Deep in man's psyche are three sacred impulses implanted by Great Nature. Despite this, modern man has lost almost completely the sacred impulse to self-perfect and also, the impulse for self-preservation has now weakened in him considerably.

- Self-Preservation
- Reproduction
- Self-Perfection

Self-Preservation:

This impulse in no longer strongly defined in modern-day terrestrial peoples. The reasons for its decline are manifold; with perhaps not a single defining reason. Contributing factors are cities, police, modern social habits and the decline in man's natural instincts. It manifests in many different forms... castles, lake-dwellings, tree-houses, weapons, the emergence of martial arts etc. We have developed very sophisticated methods of self-defence, using many different kinds of weapons, both old and new.

Today it can be said that this facet of man's psyche is not as well developed in us, as it was in ancient times. We now rely on *someone else to protect us*; the police, the army, the Guardian Angels and even on occasions, our neighbour. We generally do not take much time to develop self-defence skills or instincts, partly because of the speed and tempo of modern living ('we do not have the time'), and partly due to our attitudes towards these issues – we now let the police handle our day-to-day safety.

Reproduction:

This sacred impulse is present in almost all terrestrial beings, starting very young and manifesting strongly upon reaching puberty.

Sex is the strongest modern-day impulses in terrestrial beings. So much so, that everyone tries to exploit this facet of man's nature. Sex or reproductive instinct may be present, while the instinct of self-preservation may be absent.

Sex today has, in many ways, become a commodity – this is the problem. Sex is now used from advertising ladies accessories to the biggest blockbuster movies. Sex when used in this way becomes 'infra-sexuality'. On the other hand, 'supra-sexuality', which is the refusal to use sex in these banal and crude ways, is the mature and intelligent approach to sexuality; i.e. the rejection of pornography.

From the esoteric perspective, sex energy is both 'man's chief form of slavery and his chief potential for higher development': sex energy is one of the prime forces in the inner alchemical process, which allows a human being to transcend his own mortality. But this ancient and secret science is unknown to modern man. Today, alchemy is viewed as a crazy medieval science, working on metals.

Self-Perfection:

The last of the three sacred impulses for man on our list, happens to be the most important but also the one which is most atrophied in men and women of today's world. The impulse for self-perfection is of paramount importance for terrestrial *three-brained-beings*. Without this impulse, there would be no hope for the people of the Earth, no hope whatever!

Under the surface of modern man's superficial consciousness is buried *the impulse to self-perfect*, but it must be stressed – *it is buried very deep*. On the surface, we project our petty superficial and sensory consciousness outward, in the form of desire and wants.

This projection of energy outward holds the key to the impulse in question. Our energy constantly projects outwards and downwards and, as the ancient alchemists have pointed out in the distant past, we become a mere medium for cosmic forces to pass through. This <u>energy pump</u> must be reversed. We cannot begin to do this without first awakening *the sacred impulse to self-perfect*.

'A person lives in his or her own very small cosmos which is his or her world and this very small world is governed mainly by self-interests. People do not yet live in this world – this small planet called the Earth. This is due to the lack of development of consciousness, as are so many of the troubles of this Earth. Consciousness, in the majority of people, is confined to a very small world of themselves and their own interests. We have scarcely any proper consciousness of one another. We can only take in what we are interested in and if a person is only interested in himself and those belonging to his own self-interests, everything said about the Cosmos has little or no meaning, for it demands a form of thinking <u>beyond oneself</u>. A person is <u>glued to his life</u> – thus he has, as a rule, very little free force in him to think beyond his immediate self-interests.'

Maurice Nicoll [36]

'HYDROGENS'

Gurdjieff introduces us to the subject of 'hydrogens': a system of calibrating energy/ matter in the entire cosmos, from the densest material to the most refined.

Energy/matter is viewed in terms of 'the Ray of Creation', a very ancient glyph of the cosmos: which in effect, shows a descending ray of intelligent energy from the Absolute to what is known as absolute void - becoming matter and then reaching a point in the universe where it reverts to return to the Absolute: creating a continuous loop of energy/matter interchange and reciprocity!

This is a most remarkable glyph or diagram, which apparently has been used in wisdom schools for thousands of years in one variation or another.

G. explains that energy projected downwards from the Absolute, in a descending octave, is highly refined and highly intelligent. Generally, in modern day life we are not au fait with the concept of 'intelligent energy'. However, as this energy passes through the stellar worlds, galaxies, to our sun, it then becomes more dense and less refined and intelligent as it passes through the planets, to our Earth and finally to the Moon and beyond to absolute void.

He tells us that lower down the cosmic scale matter has a high density, but a low vibration and low intelligence: its hydrogen calibration is quite high, an inverse ratio, an example would be food which is calibrated as H768 and psychic energy - the energy we use to think with, being H48. Thinking is more refined than food!

Further up the cosmic scale or higher in the cosmic planes, matter becomes energy of a very refined nature, and high frequency Beings or Intelligences appear on these levels.

So we can see from this, that there is a definite ratio between energy on higher cosmic levels to that of lower cosmic scales.

The higher the cosmic level, the more refined the matter, the greater the intelligence and the higher the vibratory level. By contrast, the lower in the cosmic scale, we find solid matter denser, less intelligent, with a low vibration.

'It is then necessary to think about what a hydrogen means. A hydrogen is a point in the universe regarded as a qualitative scale – namely, a scale of degrees of excellence. The lower hydrogens are manifested to our external senses as objects, as 'stones', as 'grass' as 'meat', as 'water', etc. But when this point in the universe called H48 is reached, its manifestation is only internal and so has to do with states of consciousness. Hydrogen 48 is the lowest of the so called psychic hydrogens. Our ordinary consciousness uses, as it were, hydrogen 48.'

Maurice Nicoll [37]

So we can see from the above that when we reach the refinement of Hydrogen 48, although we are in the psychic realm, we are still in duality! It is only when we connect to higher centres, which use hydrogen 12 and hydrogen 6, that we leave behind duality ... in our higher centres there are no opposites or contradictions. The higher emotional centre uses hydrogen 12 and, higher intellectual centre H6!

Here are some examples of common hydrogens: 192 - air, 348 - water, 768 - food, 1536 - Wood, and 3072 which are minerals.

One of the very interesting things about hydrogens is that we transform coarse hydrogens in our bodies upwards, into much finer hydrogens; the finest hydrogen we produce is, of course, hydrogen Si 12 or sex energy! This process or octave takes place within the body and is formed fundamentally by the combination of three hydrogens, by way of a sophisticated process – hydrogen 192 which is air, hydrogen 678 which is food and hydrogen 48 which are impressions. This process is an ascending octave or, in other words, energy/matter is transformed upwards into finer and finer materials – until hydrogen Si 12 is reached.

'... man as a living being transforms lower energy-matters into higher energy-matters. This is life. Life is transformation. Man transforms lower hydrogens into finer hydrogens.'

Maurice Nicoll [38]

The interesting point about all of this is that Man has the potential built into his very 'blueprint', to bring this hydrogen of Si 12 to a higher level still. This is one of the secrets of the ancient science of Alchemy. However, it must be understood from the outset, that mechanically, matter/energy in Man is only brought to this level of Hydrogen Si 12 and no further. That is, all the very complex digestion and other sophisticated transformations which take place in us automatically and, controlled by nature so to speak – stop at a critical juncture! We are designed by nature to go so far, and no more. However, nature has 'left the door open' if you like, to go much further along this transformational path and this is where higher learning come in – this knowledge of how Man can transform himself into a Spiritual Being; forms the secret core of all true esoteric wisdom and teachings!

In the future volumes we will continue our overview of hydrogens and, also, we will look at the subject of octaves (law of seven) and triads, (the law of three forces!)

THE 'SEVEN RINGS OF POWER'

('ONE RING TO RULE THEM ALL')

In every human being there exists a physical body and a counter part or energy body, this is sometimes called the aura or etheric body. It has seven locations or centres of power existing in its make-up and many sub-centres throughout its structure. These energy centres or 'chakras' are of vital importance to us in the field of esoteric study, since it is from these energy centres that all real power is determined in the human 'bio-machine'.

When we deal with the inner-development of man, we are in reality dealing with the development or non-development of these subtle energy centres.

These energy centres in the make-up of a terrestrial being have independent mechanisms, intelligence, vibratory levels, energy and also many subtle but vital functions to perform; both in the physical body and in the spiritual elements of an individual. Perhaps the most interesting facet of the chakras is that they are not of the physical plane but belong to the etheric plane: they exist only in our physical plane because they are anchored in the physical body.

The Seven Centres in Terrestrials are:

- Moving Centre
- Instinctive Centre
- Sex Centre
- Intellectual Centre
- Emotional Centre
- Higher Intellectual Centre
- Higher Emotional Centre

The knowledge, which we are in the process of unfolding here, comes from esoteric schools and <u>cannot be found</u> among our ordinary social inventions or theories on life.

The two higher centres (6 and 7 above), are extremely special in that, in most <u>normal</u> terrestrial peoples, they <u>are functioning</u> but <u>remain unconnected to the other five lower centres</u> which operate during the normal functioning of our organism in

71

our everyday lives.

What must be understood is that we do not just have one mind but in fact <u>many</u> <u>minds</u>! The belief that we have just one mind is an error or flaw in how we think and in how we perceive ourselves. In reality we possess seven minds!

The chakra system in humans has, in fact, been alluded to in many of the ancient and also current <u>incomplete systems of knowledge</u>. These include the Hindu, Buddhist, Tantric and Taoist materials, however a complete and full overview of the chakras is missing from the anals of history and religion and philosophy in general.

Each centre represents a different major brain function in human beings and is quite independent from the other centres in many respects. In order to learn about our inner-world, it is first necessary to learn about the chakras or centres.

<u>Central to the esoteric teaching on the energy centres is that they do not function</u> <u>according to their original design criteria – they often steal energy from one another</u> <u>and, one centre often takes over the role and function of another centre</u>!

A good example of this is our emotional centre; it operates with hydrogen 24 but should work with a much finer energy: hydrogen 12. This means that we do not live in Essence, do not understand life but merely play a part, like an actor in a silent movie – life is no longer vivid and exciting when we lose hydrogen 12 from our emotional field. How do we get hydrogen 12 into our emotional centre? The Indian philosopher and teacher Patanjali talks of this phenomenon thus:

'When you are inspired by some purpose, some extraordinary project, all your thoughts break their bounds: your consciousness expands in every direction and you find yourself to be in a new, great and wonderful world – and you discover yourself to be a greater person by far than you ever dreamed yourself to be.'

Patanjali [39]

Moving Centre

This centre controls movement in the body and such things as our physical activity, watching television etc. When for instance, one learns a new skill for the first time, let us say driving a car, the mind or intellectual centre will struggle with this challenge primarily, and then, once mastered, it passes the complete 'mechanism for driving' into moving centre for future recall. It becomes automatic and without the direct involvement of the mind.

One of the biggest problems seems to be with people differentiating between moving-centre functions and instinctive-centre functions. The main difference being as follows: our instinctive-centre functions are inborn … such as digestion, heartbeat and our immune system etc, whereas our moving-centre functions or manifestations have to be learned.

Instinctive Centre

This brain function controls all of our instinctive functions, such as fear of heights, instinctive movements and instinctive reactions to many situations, people or even places. This includes our so called inner 'hunches', the functioning of our organs, breathing and circulation of the blood.

Sex Centre

This brain function controls our sexual drive, our passion or lack of it. Our sex Centre works on very fine energy, hydrogen si 12; much finer than that of, say, our moving centre or intellectual centre. This centre, too, is different from the others in that it does not positive or negative halves. Thus, there is no such thing as negative sex.

Intellectual Centre

The intellectual centre controls our thoughts and our reasoning. Our centres will sometimes swap their functions for that of another, for instance, thinking centre will often take over or substitute for our emotional centre and vice versa. Moving centre will often step in for intellectual centre for a time and so on. This swapping of functions can, if it is maintained on a prolonged basis, render the person imbalanced or, what modern psychology terms neurotic or dysfunctional.

Under certain specific circumstances, when for instance one is reading and also simultaneously preoccupied with something else, moving centre will take over the function of reading – in a mechanical fashion. Where, for instance, we are vocally reading aloud, we will continue to do so, as before, but in a crude mechanical way, our tone of voice being audibly different.

Emotional Centre

This particular brain function controls our feelings. Our feelings work with a very strong and 'explosive' energy, many times more refined than our mental centre.

Under ordinary conditions of life, we have <u>no control</u> over our emotional centre and we have only very little control over our instinctive centre. For example, <u>we cannot</u> be angry or glad without cause and the cause <u>is usually</u> an external one. In other words, our emotional and instinctive centres are controlled mainly externally; by outside stimuli.

N.B. Our <u>negative emotions</u> originate in the emotional centre; but this centre does not have a negative function to it – <u>as ordained by nature</u>. Strictly speaking, it is formed by 'an artificial graft' attached to the emotional centre from early childhood. To express negative emotions means to lose vast amounts of our precious psychic energy from that centre!

Higher Emotional and Higher Intellectual Centres (6 and 7)

These centres are fully functional in all normal people but <u>are not connected</u> to the lower centres. This by analogy is rather like a huge power plant fully operational and functioning but not hooked-up to the power grid. This means that, in each normal human being, the potential exists for a powerful alliance between the incredibly powerful higher centres and the five lower ones.

The two higher centres, unlike the lower centres described, possess a vast psychic potential for higher-consciousness in humans. <u>The problem being that our lower centres are undeveloped and also not functioning as they should</u> in order to facilitate such a connection.

Before such a connection can be made, the lower centres require 'adjusting and cleansing' in a specific way; otherwise a premature *amalgam of forces* would prove disastrous!

The ideas relating to the seven Chakras in human beings is very old; in fact it comes from remote antiquity – from esoteric schools and before the dawn of history. It must be understood that the division of our brain into seven definitive centres or functions cannot be discovered in any ordinary way.

When we are instructed with regard to the division of centres in human beings, we may even observe them in ourselves with some difficulty and find that this division is true; the reality is, ordinary mind cannot discover their existence unaided or by itself – nor by research! Modern science clearly shows us this!

It must further be understood that each of the five lower energy centres, with the exception of the sex centre, is divided into three parts: higher, lower and middle. Each of these three parts are then subsequently divided in three; giving nine divisions in all. The higher part of the centre represents the highest intelligence of that particular centre: the middle part represents its dynamic energy, and the lower represents its mechanical part, its formative function.

Inner-power comes from accessing the higher parts of our energy centres; this feat requires effort on our part, attention and connecting to our emotional function. Another way of looking at it, is that, deep pondering on our situation, qualities and our life, requires us to use the higher parts of centres and, most importantly, more than one centre. We are required to go beyond ourselves, our often narrow and self-centred agenda, our small repertoire of thoughts and limited parameters of awareness and knowledge.

Another facet of all of this is that, we must also use the higher parts of centres if we are ever to develop integrity! The middle or mechanical parts of centres can only inform personality; only the higher parts of centres can form Essence in us and thus real integrity!

It is important to note also, that 'knowing' comes from the use of one centre, but understanding comes from engaging at least three centres and, the higher parts of these three centres! Here I refer to the intellectual knowing of something mostly by memory; which is the function of the intellectual centre but to understand something is quite a different order of cognition, this means that we perceive not only the subject matter but all that is connected to it on many diverse levels! We, if you like, see 'the big picture' in relation to the subject matter: it is not taken in isolation and, we also perceive the inner-nature of the subject observed.

From the general perspective, most people in society only use the lower parts of centres. This is, for the most part, the result of wrong education in the collective: 'education' causes this disjunction in a person between 'knowing' intellectually and understanding – only the development of the latter in a human being is of value. Thus we have vast numbers of people whose cognitive ability is muted: the emotional function in the person is neglected giving the individual 'a two dimensional view of life'. In ancient times, when authentic knowledge relating to man's condition was prevalent – this condition of modern man would have been considered shameful. We have become 'cognitively dwarfed'!

At the beginning of this section I mentioned the 'seven rings of power' and 'one ring to rule them all' This, of course, refers to the seven chakras in man. When the two higher chakras or centres are united with the five lower, we then have a person of higher Being. <u>Seven chakras become one</u>! One meta-chakra, with seven inner dynamics. This is what 'one ring to rule them all' really means.

CONSCIENCE

Although many people believe the contrary, Conscience is not present in ordinary people. Instead, it is mostly 'crusted over' and encased by our False-Personality and buffers! <u>It does not function in us as it was originally created in us</u>!

What exactly is <u>Conscience</u>?

It can be understood as <u>objective morality</u> in us! As Conscience begins to 'wake up' in us, we experience it in a strange and sometimes painful fashion we become aware of many psychological and emotional elements within us that we formerly ignored or suppressed!

Conscience is an 'emotional field', in which we experience all our inner feelings at once; all our inner and outer contradictions, all our weaknesses and failings become apparent to us in one super-cognitive moment. This moment can extend often for hours or even days at the beginning as Conscience <u>begins to manifest</u> in us!

Buffers or the filters in Man's psyche which block his perceptions of Truth about himself and life, prevent Conscience from manifesting naturally. That is why, it will on occasions happen, that the individual sustains a shock and these buffers are temporarily rendered passive; then the person experiences Conscience fully! This shock may be a bereavement, a near death experience, a serious illness or some other type of unexpected shock sustained in life! The result is often the same!

When, in the conditions of ordinary life, Conscience begins to manifest in a person, the usual reaction in such a person is to 'shut it down' very rapidly; simply because it is, to begin with, a very uncomfortable feeling.

<u>Conscience, in the beginning is a very uncomfortable feeling</u>!

Conscience, unlike subjective morality, is a constant factor; a stable datum. That is to say, either there is a manifestation of Conscience or there is not; it is always the same for each and every individual. Conscience can also be described as a type of super-charged emotional experience, and a subtle, silent explosion of understanding in relation to our relationships with others. Conscience for example, is the same for a person in the U.K, as it is for a person in Central Africa!

Conscience exists deep within every normal person; it is a state <u>where we cannot hide anything from ourselves</u>! It helps us understand what is good and what is bad in our conduct towards others and, of course, also our conduct in relation to ourselves;

missed opportunities, bad behaviour, stubbornness, situations where we manifest a lack of tact towards others, arguments, moods, a lack of trust, over confidence, crude mistakes, undermining behaviour, ego-centric manifestations, being smug, etc, etc.

However, it is also much more than this; it also related to <u>where our life is going</u> and if we are satisfied with our life in general?

<u>Conscience manifests slowly at first</u> in 'short bursts' and requires time and inner-work to fully manifest it in our psyche. This done, Conscience becomes our friend and mentor.

Why is Conscience uncomfortable at first?

It is uncomfortable because we see ourselves for what we really are, without any of the usual pleasantries or illusions. It also shows us very clearly, in a powerful emotional fashion, what is wrong in our lives! (Accelerated emotional cognition.)

Acquired Conscience

It is important to distinguish between genuine Conscience and 'acquired conscience'. Acquired conscience is all those social habits and traits a person acquires from their culture – schooling, religion, political affiliation, class, manners, background, parents, country of origin, status etc, - all of which are <u>mechanically absorbed</u> from their surroundings. These habits and traits are always subjective and, of course, are different in different peoples.

An example of this acquired conscience is where an individual will openly give to the poor, in full view of his friends as it were, in order to create an impression of philanthropy and generosity; this is called 'to be seen of men' and is not a manifestation of genuine Conscience! Real Conscience acts in private and is not concerned with what others think or, about how much praise one will attract!

'Tradition forms an acquired conscience in us and is stronger than individual contact with a person. <u>Tradition makes you not yourself</u>. You have traditional 'I's in you that are acquired, which make it very difficult for you to become a real person, a real individual, free to communicate with everyone, and so it narrows down your relationship to people.
'… Now acquired conscience is always connected with self-love, which continually puffs itself up into all forms of vanity, all forms of making difficulties, of duty, etc. based on prestige, tradition, honor, nationality, and so on. In this way self-love incites continual antagonism, war, violence and so on.'

Maurice Nicoll [40]

LYING IN MAN

'The psychology of man is the psychology of lying.'

P.D. Ouspensky

The subject of lying in contemporary man is a fascinating subject and is in fact a complete study in itself, within the overall remit of esoteric psychology.

This issue has so many ramifications for both the inner and outer life of man, that we can but cover some of the more obvious issues involved. G. tells us that lying begins by saying 'I know', when one does not know and cannot know! Lying is strengthened and accentuated by the 'psychological landscape' created by modern education! It is very interesting to notice this false 'psychological-landscape' produced in people through our pseudo-educational system and how it retards the very fabric of the individuals' cognitive range. This, but one factor!

The core element involved is the presumption that the person is aware of all the important facets of life and living, through our current 'educational' modalities. The person having completed their 'educational' studies, leaves school or college with the presumption that they have received 'gold standard' tuition and are in the vanguard of intellectual and educational standards anywhere in the world.

The truth is in reality, somewhat different; modern 'education' is really a form of very subtly imposed ignorance. That which is missing is much larger than that which has been learned! People are duped by a seamless system of deception and complex lies! We are fed 'a diet' of half-truths and vacuous info!

However, it would seem that this deception is not conscious or planned but it is rather, a now omnipresent feature of the psyche of man: the truth is that man's cognitive ability has been downgraded over time, without our awareness! On the other hand, it suits the powers that be, not to have a race of super-aware people. People have no idea that all of the truly important aspects of higher terrestrial knowledge have not even been touched upon, in their 'education' … below are but a few examples:

- Cosmic laws governing man's life on the Earth (there are many)
- Esoteric psychology (begins where modern psychology ends!)
- The true ancient history of planet Earth (unknown to modern Man)
- Man's hidden potentialities (never really explored by modern science)
- The secrets behind the ancient science of Alchemy (unknown to us)

- The core teachings behind all religions (outside man's cognitive range)
- The gradual decline of our biosphere (just starting to wake up to)
- The dwindling of man's cognitive abilities over the past 5,000 years!
- The vast array of defects in modern 'education' (a type of arrogance)
- The very structure and modus operandi of contemporary culture causes mental illness in countless people worldwide (unknown to sociology)
- The dangers relating to pharmaceutical medicines and the fact that many medical procedures are, in reality, unnecessary!
- The Great Ways that once existed upon the Earth (Man is ignorant of)
- The necessity of working on two lines of development in ourselves, at once: Knowledge and Being (modern people unaware of line of Being)
- The fact that our being attracts our life! (real Law of Attraction)
- The vast extent of lying in contemporary man, has rendered society as a healthy, holistic and harmonious entity - invalid. (unknown to modern sociology and psychology)
- Man lives in a definitive quality of duality he can never escape from; under the conditions of ordinary life; joy and sorrow, love and hate, anger and calm, etc (modern man has no concept of his potential for oneness)
- The extent of deception in governments and large institutions worldwide
- Higher Knowledge relating to life and the inner development of Man; if encountered by contemporary peoples – is quickly forgotten! (not understood by contemporary peoples and retention also a problem)
  Another real consequence of the dwindling of Man's cognitive abilities!

The very nature and corrosive effect of modern Man's societies - which today include pornography, crass consumerism, endemic lying and deception, pseudo-educational modalities, superficial politicians who lie, narrow self-interest, subtle government deception, crude and profit oriented medical practices, low level mental illness in large sections of our communities – all of which, to name but a few, serve to weaken the very spiritual fabric of the individual! In other words, all those customs, modalities and practices known to the ancient peoples of the Earth and all of which, served to strengthen and increase wellbeing, cognitive range, community spirit etc, these are now replaced by negative and harmful social habits and a raft of crude interests and pseudo social activities.

The damage sustained by the individual because of our socially deviant activities and the damaging use of certain contemporary technologies lies just outside the cognitive range of most modern peoples! Many deviant and dangerous technologies are allowed for common usage, simply because of the duplicity and cunning of those who produce and profit from them! <u>In other words – people are unaware that they are damaged daily simply by what surrounds them</u>! Lying and deception damages the most spiritually intimate part of a person – Essence! This is the spiritual seed in man.

So, we can see from the above, that lying plays a much bigger role in the life of man, than is normally recognised. In fact, lying has an enormous corrosive impact on every aspect of human life.

We will consider further ramifications and pertinent elements relating to lying in modern man, in volume 2 of this current series of materials.

THE EARTH AS A 'BIOLOGICAL PRISON'

Unfortunately for modern man, because of the reduction of his life principle to 'Itoclanoz' and the abnormal conditions of external life on almost all parts of the Earth, his life and inner-suffering now resembles that of a biological prison more than anything else. Gurdjieff describes the Earth as a 'pain factory'. (The real nemesis to our suffering on Earth, is 'Self-Remembering'.)

Man does not recognise this because of his conditioning and also, because of his 'narrow world horizon' which has supplanted the natural being-impulses to self-perfect and go beyond culture-bound reasoning. Gurdjieff called this – 'the terror of the situation'.

'Freedom leads to freedom. Those are the first words of truth. You do not know what is truth because you do not know what freedom is. All the truth that you know today is only 'truth' in quotation marks. <u>There is another truth, but it is not theoretical: it cannot be expressed in words, only those who have realised it in themselves can understand that truth</u>.

The freedom I speak about is the freedom that is the goal of all schools, all religions, of all times. And, in truth, that freedom can be a very great one!'

Gurdjieff [41]

The only way to escape 'prison Earth' is to pursue Truth at all costs and at every opportunity. And, of course, this is very difficult, since our culture and society is based upon lies and half-truths! We are instantly at a disadvantage. It requires that we go contrary to our conditioning; we must look at everything afresh and question everything, question all those things we formerly took for granted. <u>Although the Earth is incredibly beautiful it also possesses a dark side</u>!

Remember, even how we think, how we perceive things, is highly conditioned and is in no ways objective! We need <u>an objective template</u> – esoteric Knowledge!

Ultimately, when we engage/study esoteric materials and principles seriously, our cognitive ability begins to change radically – we are no longer 'taken in' by outward appearances; by the lies, half-truths and 'the shadow world' we are all surrounded by. <u>This is not achieved by an academic approach to esotericism</u>! It requires 'study from the heart'; an opening of the perceptions!

As we are, we cannot perceive the Earth as a biological prison: it requires a <u>definitive adjustment</u> of our cognitive ability. This adjustment is really possible and sits just one level above our present cognitive state – if you like, it is always 'awaiting our arrival'. <u>We cannot escape from that which we cannot see</u>! So, the first prerequisite is that we become aware of our true cosmic position; i.e. become aware of our tenuous position on Earth and the need for real inner-work!

Once we begin to study objectively, our true situation on planet Earth as human beings, things change radically; we find ourselves surrounded by 'well crafted' illusions and seamless complex-lies, illusions and half-truths that we have 'bought-into' throughout our life – we have never questioned the status quo!

DYSFUNCTIONS IN THE EMOTIONAL CENTRE

Because of man's abnormal existence in today's artificial societies, many natural functions in his psychology have gone astray. Cardinal among these is the dysfunction of his emotional centre. Today man can best be described as a negative entity, with negative moods, manifestations and anger dominating his psyche.

It is of such importance, that it requires a specific mention here. Many people in life just accept negativity, anger, violence, moods, as part of life and part of what they must put up with. Indeed, in relationships this is very true. However, what is not understood is that the negative part of the emotional centre is not a natural construct. In other words, there is no natural function in the emotional centre which is inherently negative. It does not exist. What actually happens is that an artificial graft is formed in this energy centre, by what is called mimicry or the influence of others being negative around you. This starts in childhood!

It is one of the most important malfunctions of modern man's psyche. One which has created a type of hell for the modern individual.

One of the central tasks for the novice to Esoteric Work is the cleansing and purification of the emotional centre. This requires careful study and diligent awareness. A specific understanding of what this means for the individual and all its ramifications, which by the way are many and deep, is required by those who seek to elevate their Knowledge and their Being. The deepening of Essence cannot be achieved without this work. <u>Our emotions carry the key to our inner evolution</u>! Our emotions are anchored in our Essence.

'Negative emotions easily attract us. People get to enjoy them. There is a story that an Angel visited the earth. He could not understand what they were enjoying. After a time the Angel got infected also. He began to enjoy negative emotions and became mad like the rest. A messenger was sent down to inform him that he had failed in his test. He had forgotten something and now must remain on the earth until he had disentangled himself from all his negative emotions, and that made him more mad than ever.'

Maurice Nicoll [42]

This shows the nature of negative emotions; they act like a contagion in society and spread in a viral fashion from person to person. Gurdjieff explains 'we have the right not to be negative'. Negative emotions really only bring great suffering. We must work to disarm negative reactions in our psyche!

Manifestations and Secondary Manifestations of an Imbalanced Emotional Centre

- Emotional outbursts/the Dark God or Goddess
- Projecting ... 'You are a very negative person'
- Often a very negative person will project their own condition
- Undermining behaviour
- Sabotage and self-sabotage
- Selective amnesia
- Lying/avoiding emotionally painful truths!
- Cloaking: hiding emotional dysfunction from others
- Jealousy
- Moodiness
- Anger/violence
- Spitefulness and grudges
- Certain types of manipulation
- Certain types of undermining behaviour
- Controlling behaviour (being a 'control freak')
- Certain addictions i.e. to food; overeating
- Noticeable negative reactions in a person to small things
- 'Fear Thinking' - thinking from a fear-based mid-set
- Neurosis
- Certain types of insecurity
- Hatred
- Impatience
- Self-pity

WORK ON NEGATIVE EMOTIONS

NEGATIVE STATES AND THE RESULTING CHAIN-REACTIONS:
(Moods, Negativity, Anger and Resentment)

- Blame Surfaces
- Big Picture of Life Disappears
- Lying Begins
- A Feeling of Being Wronged
- Understanding Ceases or Diminishes
- Moving into Mechanical or Lower Parts of Centres
- Hatred Builds
- Revenge Comes into the Equation
- Internal Considering Begins
- Person Ceases to be Reasonable
- False-Personality or Superficial-Self Emerges
- Compromise Often Disappears
- Double Standards are Often Apparent
- 'I am Right and You are Wrong' syndrome
- Other People become the Enemy
- Collective Energy-Field changes to Negative Energy

'A man cannot advance a single step in his own development unless he begins to observe and contend with evil emotions. All evil emotions – that is, all negative emotions – are useless. Each of them has its own poison. At the bottom of all these emotions lie violence and self-worship. The emotional centre, which should conduct the influences of the work to us continually, save for brief periods which we have to endure, cannot do this if it is dominated by evil emotions. If the emotional centre gives nothing save negative states, if it continually feeds us with different combinations of these negative states, it stands in the way of any possible growth of Being, of which we might otherwise be capable. It is a good thing to make lists of negative emotions for yourselves. In these states you must include various states of depression, various kinds of self-pity, various kinds of persisting resentment, of feeling badly treated, and you must also include many kinds of hatred, man unpleasant kinds of self-satisfaction and contempt of others, and especially must you include the feeling of meritoriousness, one of the most unclean of all emotions and one which perhaps shuts out all influences from Higher Centres more than any other emotion. The purification of the emotional centre is especially emphasized in the Work.'

Maurice Nicoll [43]

THE THREE LEVELS OF KARMA

• The Karma of parental influences
• The Karma from the influences of friends
• The karma of cultural influences

Definition of Karma: Every real effect must always and everywhere strive to re-enter its own cause!

The Karmic Influence From Parents

There are, of course, both positive and negative karmic effects from most parents. However, the karmic effect of parents depends on the actual quality of those parents. This will determine many pivotal elements in their children!

Negative Karma

This type of karma pertains to such items as: expectations, manipulation, pressure at school originating from parents, fear of one or both of one's parents, wrong ideas about life passing from parents to child etc, etc.

This type of karma can and does have a strong adverse effect on young people. Many young people develop psychological problems or personality disorders as a result of negative parental pressure. Unfortunately, this negative parental pressure often comes from defective or logical thinking and is very often fear based. A chain of this type of thinking and behaviour is often passed down through generation after generation in certain families!

Other forms of negative parental karma include parents deserting their children at a young age: teaching their children wrong values for life and physical, emotional and sexual abuse.

There are also sometimes more direct parental karmic effects in the form of heredity traits and tendencies transferred to the individual. These can vary from alcoholic tendencies, violence and depression to physical traits and disposition.

Positive Karma

Then, of course, there is the positive karma from parents; where parents have brought up their children with wisdom, love, dignity and understanding. In some respects also, parents will have separated their children from negative influences through wisdom, positive communication and by example! Lastly, the transfer of this wisdom and understanding to their children at every stage of their development is of vital importance.

There is, of course, one major caveat here; what most parents today consider wisdom, positive communication and example, are simply not so!

The Karmic Influence of Friends

The karmic influence of friends, especially for young people, should not be underestimated.

Obviously, much influence exerted by friends on young people is positive, but in some cases, there can be negative karma. The negative influence can sometimes continue right through childhood, adolescence and into adulthood! On some occasions, the pattern of a person's life may be changed for the worse by the adverse influence of peers.

Some obvious examples are: the use of illegal drugs, alcohol, smoking, negative attitudes, pornography and violence.

There are also many more, subtler negative influences transferred to children by their peers. These may include negative modes of thinking, addictive negative emotions and less obvious behavioural manifestations such as laziness, apathy and neglect of personal health and wellbeing.

In some cases, mental health problems can be traced all the way back to a single incident occurring while a young person was in the company of peers – e.g. while engaged in experimental drug use or the like.

Another facet of the karmic influence of friends is that of our mind-set: i.e. the mind-set we adopt for life. This includes our attitudes, emotional stances, prejudices, emotional-anchors etc.

The Karmic Influences of One's Culture

The karmic effects on our life and mind-set from our culture are substantial, significant and all pervasive.

Every culture which has existed on Earth and indeed every epoch had its own mind-set or world view. According to esotericism, our present epoch represents a 'low water-mark' in terms of culture, vision, hypocrisy, shallowness and banality.

Our world vision is narrow, trite, conceited and pregnant with cynical thinking! In our modern culture, the mode of peoples thinking, the way people view life, is a direct product of their environment; their culture. People no longer think for themselves. Man has been robbed of this ability by a vacuous culture; one which perpetuates false values, greed, false-interests, destruction, exploitation and violence … all cloaked in fine words!

INTEGRITY

The astute study of esoteric psychology allows us to extrapolate a certain critical understanding; a crucial pivotal insight into man's 'inner-landscape' – <u>his real inner-world</u>!

Esoteric psychology begins where terrestrial psychology ends. <u>Mr Gurdjieff tells us that all contemporary psychology is 'childish'</u>! He was 100% correct.

Contemporary psychology deals mainly with illness in man and the paradigm of restoring people to 'balanced mental and emotional health': within an already maladjusted society. This mode: helping people to '<u>function well</u>' in a deranged and <u>emotionally-corrosive environment</u>, cannot be held in high esteem – <u>one must go beyond the illusion of a normal and helpful society</u>, which is cohesive and harmonious … there to be integrated into 'at all costs'.

That is not to say that our mental and emotional health is not important, however, attempting to integrate into a vacuous and maladjusted society can only result in more emotional and psychological trauma – long term.

How can it be possible to gain balance and inner-synergy by wedding oneself to such a fractured and banal cultural socioscape – this is quite impossible. <u>It is the very structure and fabric of our maladjusted society itself, which causes mental illness and unnecessary conflict in our life – but this is hidden from us by the powerful programming we are continually subject to from childhood</u>!

This was known by the great Sufi teachers of old: when they stated that all that existed in the Cosmos, had structure and a modus operandi, and that we, in our societies, must emulate <u>cosmic order</u> – otherwise mankind would suffer and degrade beyond our imagination. <u>This was no casual remark or observation</u>!

This is another gaping omission and 'blind spot' in contemporary psychology and psychiatry! The <u>very structure</u> and <u>modus operandi</u> of our current society <u>are never taken into account</u> – when looking at the causes of mental illness in populations. Modern man's perception is void in many ways, when it comes to reviewing his own social cohesion and interaction – he always settles for the status-quo. Without adequate and penetrating perception there is no way of challenging the anaemic rationale behind most modern social theories and banal sociology. <u>He has no 'measuring stick'</u> – no objective frame of reference; since his little 'bag of knowledge' is based on modern academia and his perception muted by the definitive dwindling of his cognitive ability over centuries! <u>The result is predictable and shows how Man goes in circles</u>!

Because of contemporary man's very limited cognitive range; he no longer perceives many issues which are really crucial for his own development and mode of living! These crucial issues, which remain for the most part, outside his perception – subsequently damage him. <u>In reality, the very issue of our social structure and integrity, directly impacts the integrity of the individual</u>! Man is a reflection of his environment and under the ordinary conditions of life cannot escape its unrelenting influences! Thus the 'societal diseases' of lack of integrity; lying, lack of cohesion, duplicity, superficiality, lack of vision and diminished cognitive range <u>are also found in the individual</u>! What is humorous is that each separate individual considers themselves exempt – in some way special.

Man hides and tries to camouflage his shortcomings and painful character defects by adopting the social veneer of sincerity, patience, reliability and colourful respectability. While in a different environment he often quickly drops this act to reveal a dangerous predator or perhaps a quiet, fearful, childlike creature.

Should we <u>take the individual out of a modern socioscape, early in childhood</u> before the poisonous elements of modern living can shape that psyche and place him in a more <u>natural society</u>, such as pre-invasion Tibet, we would see a person of a very different stature mature into adulthood – with no dichotomy in his psyche or manifestations: no matter what environment you place him in afterwards, the individual would remain balanced and emotionally mature! Gurdjieff tells us that pre-invasion Tibet represented the most natural, balanced and cohesive culture on the Earth, in contemporary times!

In order to protect himself from the <u>destructive influences</u> in society, the smart individual must isolate himself from them; through the use of a higher and definitive type of knowledge – <u>only through expanding our cognitive range, can we truly appreciate the need to do this</u>! Throughout history we can see many such examples of spiritual visionaries, individuals who actually expanded their cognitive range; who created communities split-off from mainstream cultures. This, to protect their followers from the dangerous and corrosive effects of what they could <u>clearly see all around them</u>.

What became clear to these visionaries is that <u>one cannot solve societal problems by the use of the same kind of thinking which created them in the first place</u>! In other words, <u>through the same cognitive level</u> of perception!

What is Integrity?

The presence of integrity in the individual is a direct co-relationship between sincerity in the person (not lying or being devious) and the person's actions: the person acting according to their word.

There is also a co-relationship between a person's knowledge and their Being development, connected with the subject of integrity. Without Being having matured and developed in the individual; there can be no true integrity! The first stages of Being development in the person, are, of course, those positive qualities such as sincerity, honesty, humility, courage, sensitivity, tenacity etc, which the individual 'distils from life' and 'forges' into their own character!

It must be noted here for the sake of completeness, that no work on evolving positive qualities and traits in the individual can progress alone: one must also work at removing negative habits, negative emotions and negative qualities at the same time!

This is why Being-development in man is vital and overrides all other factors! Integrity obviously is multi-faceted and has many other manifested sides, depending of life situations, but the core element is that of Being-development in the individual.

Other Sides to Integrity

As we can see from the diagrams A3, A4 and A5, at the end of this short volume; Personality, the False-Ego and Acquired Conscience, Integrity is the aim of ordinary people – it cannot be taken for granted. In general, the collective lack integrity but never admit to it! With most people it is a very pale phenomenon.

What does integrity mean in practice?

Integrity means the individual has developed strong and positive principles and values internally. These values and principles have been strongly forged in life and anchored in Essence - they can only be created through 'fire' or conscious suffering and effort! Such qualities found in Personality means that the person lacks integrity! Generally speaking Personality blocks the growth of integrity!

Integrity means they do not 'sell out' their principles when threatened, bribed or when fake kudos is heaped upon them by dubious social entities, people or organisations.

This means, not following the path of least resistance when one encounters a moral dilemma: perhaps crude societal pressure or manipulation, then great courage is required, because often we will find ourselves standing alone!

What is the test of integrity in a person?

A good example of integrity in an individual is, where a person is threatened verbally by another, without justification, and where the person thus accosted, refuses to be blackmailed or coerced. This is something called 'moral force'! There are indeed many facets with regards integrity; one of which is <u>not taking advantage of others</u>, even though a situation arises where it is very possible.

There are many people who behave in a correct and responsible fashion 'under the gaze of society' but, just as soon as they find themselves outside the scrutiny of their usual controlled environment, behave criminally and without restraint in relation to others! This, of course, demonstrates a complete lack of integrity. <u>The individual with integrity would help others, without hesitation, in such a situation!</u> Integrity is a precursor to our development of Conscience!

It would serve <u>the student well to ponder these ideas in relation to integrity, for they form a very important element of esoteric thought</u>. To do this, we need to raise the level of our mentation, away from habitual modes of thinking and also become aware of how our thinking is naive and moulded by cultural influences.

One of the building blocks of real integrity is the active study of esoteric ideas!

To study esoteric principles correctly, we need to alter the mode of our normal thinking, to increase its range and veracity: the only way we can really do this is by bringing our emotional function into the equation. We must begin to feel what we know or have emotions in relation to what we are learning – this brings a new 'emotional-field' into play. Our emotional function creates a new depth and connective-paradigm in relation to our study. This function is really imperative, since our emotional function works 30,000 times faster than the mechanical part of the intellectual function. It increases our cognitive ability vastly and allows us entry into the esoteric world of 'electric ideas' and new transformative knowledge – wisdom which has the power to transform a person. <u>Only a true 'living wisdom' has the power to take us beyond the mind</u>!

Mostly, people carry <u>a fake integrity</u>, one which they 'clone' from their culture or environment. This <u>cloned integrity has no substance</u> and such a person may let their friends down 'at the drop of a hat' or, desert their neighbour in their 'hour of need'. Then, this action is 'rationalised' by the mind and subsequently justified! (Obviously, there are many exceptions to this rule.)

'Every one of you is limited in his or her thinking. Of course, you do not see this yet. For some reason or other, we already think we have all points of view, all possible thoughts. This

is utterly wrong. Each one of you is limited completely and totally by the small range of thinking that you have acquired by your mental prejudices, attitudes, and so on. Life appears to you as it does because of your mental level.'

Maurice Nicoll [44]

MAN'S TRUE INNER PSYCHOLOGY

In order to change one's inner-being, it is first necessary to know the true structure of man's inner-psychology. This cannot be found in the accounts of modern psychology, lectures or books. However, it does form part of the ancient teachings of the Earth and is passed down to us through time, in the form of esoteric teachings. This is a type of meta-psychology known to the ancients!

To understand man's true inner-psychology requires a new way of thinking. It also requires a new valuation of all that we thought we previously knew!

If we remain rooted in logic and within the limits of culture-bound mentation, we cannot approach the new concepts esotericism provides us with. With esotericism comes a whole new paradigm of thought, a vast new world horizon and a movement away from narrow societal cognitive constraints!

When we are born we come into being with pure essence internally. There is nothing of the external world there yet … everything is our own and natural. But to survive in a complex and sometimes dangerous world we must develop personality. Personality enables us to cope with an ever-changing array of circumstances around us in ordinary life. Personality, however, surrounds essence, just like the shell of a nut surrounds the nut. Essence is encased by personality. Only essence can evolve. Personality is limited in its evolution because it constitutes only one or two centres (chakras) in man, and in order to develop all seven energy centres must develop in unison. (See diagrams at the rear of this manual, for a deeper understanding of esoteric psychology.)

> 'The breeze at dawn has secrets to tell you.
> Don't go back to sleep.
> You must ask for what you really want –
> Don't go back to sleep.
> People are going back and forth
> Across the door where the two worlds meet:
> The door is open and round,
> Don't go back to sleep.'
>
> Rumi [45]

In addition to these two pivotal elements in man's being, essence and personality, there is a third element; that of the false-ego or superficial-self.

The false-ego forms part of an individual's personality and it is completely false, superficial and subsists on fantasy and lies. In many modern people this false-ego is very well defined. This pernicious and poisonous element of a person's personality prevents one seeing oneself and gives us a very wrong picture of what we are. It blocks all authentic human development!

It requires a very specific training to separate from this artificial element in our make-up. All authentic esoteric work is initially focused on this delicate issue!

The Admixture of Elements in a Man's Being

It must be understood, that in the average person on the street, these three elements are mixed in a person's Being and manifestations. They are not differentiated. In order for a person to develop internally or spiritually, it is first necessary to separate from the false-ego and then, render personality passive, while rendering essence active. This is a definitive process and requires time and effort to achieve.

It is only the ancient teachings of esotericism which show us the way and gives us means of doing so!

'A man must first understand certain things. He has thousands of false conceptions, chiefly about himself and he must get rid of some of them before beginning to acquire anything new.'
Gurdjieff [46]

The Three Reversals:

The first reversal possible in the psyche of man is that of reversing the function and juxtaposition of Essence and Personality – thereby making Essence active and Personality passive. Ordinarily in man – Personality is the active force.

The second reversal is that of viewing life from the perspective of esoteric ideas and not as is usual for us: viewing esoteric ideas from the moulded ideas we have accumulated from ordinary life.

Separation from the False-Ego or False-Consciousness: Without separation from the false-ego, work on our Being will prove very slow and difficult. This process of separation is one of the keys to inner-freedom!

The third reversal is 'Self-Remembering' or 'the Witnessing Consciousness'. This is the third level of consciousness possible for Man. There is also a fourth level of consciousness; namely Objective Consciousness which the Buddhists call Nirvana and the Hindu's, Sat-Chit-Annanda!

ESSENCE, PERSONALITY AND THE FALSE-EGO

Firstly it must be understood that one cannot find this Knowledge in contemporary society ... it does not exist there. Modern psychology said Gurdjieff 'lacks substance'! It is necessary to have a thirst for Truth and a strong desire to access Wisdom; whatever the obstacles.

If a person is satisfied with his or her life, then there is no enquiry, there is no search for Truth; for real meaning in life. Real meaning does not exist in ordinary life; ordinary life cannot be explained in terms of itself! It can only be explained and real meaning found, if life is explained from a higher perspective; from a Knowledge outside of life …. one has to be able 'to stand outside' and 'look back at life'.

Esoteric Knowledge is our legacy. It has been handed down to those of us 'who have eyes to see' and 'ears to hear'! People however, do not see this wisdom nor do they want a share of it in general. They pass it over. They do not see its value. With a diminished cognitive level mankind is blind to Truth!

This wisdom of the ancients is, in reality, the single most valuable commodity on this Earth of ours. In ancient times, it was valued higher than wealth, riches or status. Nowadays, people accept the banal without any questioning!

It is necessary to have what one might call 'a healthy dissatisfaction with life and what it has to offer' before one can truly appreciate this wisdom!

'Only dead people are without discontent. A really alive person has to live his discontent. He has to be thirsty, he has to be afire. Only through that fieriness, that thirst, will he live an intense life.'

Osho [47]

A person who wishes to develop spiritually and truly grow internally must find a way to develop essence. The development of essence and the rendering of personality passive is paramount. Essence is developed at the expense of the false-ego – as Essence grows, the false-ego begins to die.

However, to do this requires a whole new approach to life, to one's psychology, to other people and to one's aspirations. To change one's inner being requires a higher order of Knowledge. Essence cannot change by itself, nor can essence change or grow through the environment and circumstances of ordinary society!

'Now Essence ceases to grow because it has not the right food from Life to grow by. Life can provide the food for the development of personality but not the food necessary for the development of Essence. <u>*The secret is that Personality and Essence need different foods for their respective development*</u>*. They need different kinds of truths. For example, the education of Personality is developed by knowledge of science, but Essence is not. A knowledge, say, of the world-markets and the political situation develops Personality, but Essence is not developed by knowing truths of this kind. Essence, before it is manifested in a human body, derived from the parents on Earth, comes from a much higher level than the Planetary World; the Solar Plane, under 24 orders of laws ... it has a very high origin ... by comparison, Personality has a very low origin in the cosmic scale ... But if a man, imbued with the Knowledge of esotericism, continually steeps his mind in its Truths and thinks and thinks again from them and perceives their depth, and acknowledges them and applies them to his inner states, essence will begin to grow.'*

Maurice Nicoll [48]

THE SUPERFICIAL-SELF OR FALSE-EGO
UNDER 96 ORDERS OF LAWS

- False pictures of oneself
- Imaginary traits and abilities we think we possess
- False pride
- Conceit
- Lacking adaptive thinking
- Internal considering … 'making accounts' – selfish behaviour
- Great difficulty in forgiving and holding grudges for a long time
- Lack of humility
- Absence of real sincerity
- The false-ego always has to be right
- Often relies on the approval or superficial praise of others!
- Decision making often based on the opinions of others!
- Lost in 'narrow self-interest' and petty pursuits
- Usually cannot suspend judgement – needs 'hard and fast proof'
- Cannot see 'the big picture' in situations – can only see immediate needs
- Often has low confidence and self-esteem
- The false-ego makes an art out of lying and often becomes a master!
- This person will often be very insecure by nature
- Prone to mental-illness
- Finds it difficult to take no for an answer, and will react negatively to same!
- Another tell-tale sign of the false-ego is 'control-freak' behaviour
- Prone to addictions – especially drugs of various kinds
- The false-ego cannot take criticism of any kind. It reacts negatively!
- A reservoir of negativity is permanently lurking beneath the surface
- <u>Often</u> a tendency to avoid physical work. 'I am too good to work!'

'To work is to free you from the absolutely erroneous ideas that you have about yourself, the absolutely wrong attitudes you have, wrong forms of imagination and all the rest of it, which contribute to form false-personality; which is your real enemy and causes you endless and useless suffering without you knowing anything about it.'

Maurice Nicoll [49]

The Superficial-self or False-Personality forms itself in an individual's personality, where an individual is surrounded by fantasy, imagination, lies and half-truths! Many modern societies perpetuate a paradigm of half-truths and complex lies! Modern education reinforces the False-Ego considerably!

One of the most common aspects of the false-ego is guilt projection. The false-ego will project its own guilt onto another and often do this very effectively. This technique of projection is very well known even to ordinary psychology.

This technique on the part of the false-ego has two major aspects. Firstly, it casts doubt completely on the other individual, undermining the person and secondly, it takes the attention off the false-ego and the real deception.

The false-ego is also very good at convincing others of the guilt and wrongdoing of its target.

The false-ego often manifests itself as the root of selfishness. It works for itself and is not interested in the well-being of the other person. On a group level, it works for the group – the family, the party, the nation – and, looking after the interests of the group, sometimes in the most dutiful way, it pays no attention to the needs of people outside that group.

The false-ego is always identified with the material world and will always place material wealth above people and right values.

The false-ego is very often physically or mentally cruel without any scruples; he can act sadistically and punish others without feeling any guilt himself.

The false-ego often uses coercion on others in order to control or manipulate them. The false-ego is often found around the world in positions of authority.

'There are many things besides negative emotions in false-personality. For instance, in false-personality there are always bad mental habits – wrong thinking. False-personality or parts of false-personality, are always based on wrong thinking. At the same time, if you were to take negative emotions away from false-personality it would collapse; it could not exist without them.'

P.D. Ouspensky [50]

QUALITIES LACKING IN THE FALSE-EGO

- Love
- Empathy
- Compassion
- True understanding

- Flexibility or adaptive thought
- Never takes all factors into account and always refuses to look deeper
- It cannot suspend judgment and keep an open mind

Being unable to see the less obvious factors involved and which need to be taken into account, it will always see two opposite sides, and take one of them – there is, as far as it can see, no alternative conclusion

- Since the false-ego is cut-off from essence and what lies behind essence: the True Self or Real 'I', it cannot make a synthesis (think psychologically) and so produce a reconciliation of two opposite views
- For the false-ego there is always the struggle between one party and another, one class and another – or one nation is right and the other wrong. Never is there the realisation of the contribution that both can make, or the real truth which lies behind each and which is being ignored
- Where a new idea is presented to it, it will feel under a compulsion immediately to accept the belief, or reject it – it does not occur to it, to delve deeper and more subtly in order to understand the real truth
- False-ego has no desire really for truth – it desires only to support its own opinions, which to it <u>are</u> truth, and for this purpose it will content itself with lies, distortions and half-truths … as long as they serve to keep its own view securely established
- It will also make great use of the emotional association of words, ignoring their basic meaning, thereby attributing meanings to them to serve its own purpose!

PERSONALITY

UNDER 48 ORDERS OF LAWS

All that an individual acquires from society: parents, friends, culture, etc. Personality is all that is acquired/artificial in an individual. Personality can easily be altered in a person. Personality is made up of many sub-personalities, each with its own opinions, interests, preferences, prejudices, etc.

All work/interest in esotericism and inner-development begins in personality but ends in essence.

In personality also, are many contradictory sub-personalities, these are the contradictions present in each person but these contradictions usually remain invisible because of <u>buffers</u>! Buffers prevent a person from noticing sometimes even huge contradictions in their lives and in their manifestations.

Personality <u>is controlled by the hypnotism of life</u>! We are always under the illusion that we are one. That we are a single unchanging entity inside … But this is nothing but a very clever illusion. Personality also gives us the illusion that we are free!

If a person remains anchored in personality, they will never truly learn <u>to think independently or think for themselves</u>! <u>To do this it is necessary to move into essence</u>! Moving into essence allows an individual to think in a new and 'three dimensional' way.

'Man is 99% social animal: one per cent himself!'

Gurdjieff [51]

Through personality come all the influences of society, both positive and negative. When a person grows internally or spiritually it is always essence which grows, becomes a soul: personality is merely a means to an end.

To be satisfied with personality is to make a grave error: personality is nothing more than a mirage. The chief characteristic of personality is that <u>it is easily controlled from outside, from external trends, fashions, beliefs in society</u>!

'Personality, developed according to your centre of gravity, will mislead and not give you the force and meaning you are seeking for. <u>It will not give substance and meaning to your life</u>.'

Maurice Nicoll [52]

'Today, when vision is ceasing, the power of external life, of machines and war, increases. Man must serve one or the other. Without vision, without the influences of conscious man, humanity is enslaved by outer life. Because it has no inner life, having given up the idea of religion, <u>it has nothing with which to resist outer life. When there is no inner life one passes into the power of outer life completely</u>. Man becomes helpless – a creature of mass-movements, mass politics, of gigantic mass-organisations.'

Maurice Nicoll [53]

Personality is shallow because it is only interested in superficial things; in externals, its viewpoint is always one-dimensional and lacks depth!

<u>Personality has to be trained in order for it to focus on what is real</u>!

'Organic life serves planetary purposes, it does not exist for itself, an individual man is a highly specialised cell in it, but on that scale an individual cell does not exist – it is too small. Our ordinary points of view are very naïve and homocentric: everything turns around man.

But man is a very insignificant thing, part of a very big machine. Organic life is a particular cosmic unit and man is a particular unit in this big mass of organic life. He has the possibility of further development, but this really depends on man's own effort and understanding. It enters into the cosmic purpose that a certain number of men should develop, but not all, for that would contradict another cosmic purpose.

But a certain number of men can escape, and also enters into the cosmic purpose.'

P.D. Ouspensky [54]

ESSENCE

UNDER 24 ORDERS OF LAWS

Essence is the core of man … what is essentially yours from birth: often an adult will have an essence of only 8 or 10 years old … others 12 or 14 years old. Also, essence may be underdeveloped i.e. may be stupid/lazy or maladjusted!

Essence is the seed which must be developed in man; it is the 'gold' which can make more 'gold'.

QUALITIES: THAT IS, IN A WELL ADJUSTED AND BALANCED ESSENCE

Primary - Sincerity, Humility, Courage and Tenacity
Secondary - Awe, a natural respect for others, dignity, pride, empathy. Also, a natural hunger for Truth and a natural impulse to help others without payment!

Quick reference guide:

- False-personality feeds on lies
- Personality feeds on 'any old story' and is identified with society, fame, fashion, politics, narrow self-interest, pleasure, kudos, social status, 'to be seen of men', etc
- Essence can only feed on Truth … essence can only grow through the reception of Truth!

DEVELOPED ESSENCE

Ordinarily, essence in a contemporary man is a very undeveloped quantum. Therefore, the development of essence in a man or woman is the primary objective; since essence is everything that is real in an individual, everything that is his or her own. Everything that is gained, is gained through essence development in the individual – this, at the expense of Personality of course.

Developing essence is not an easy objective, for if the person remains rooted in his or her 'comfort zone', or if a person is anchored in personality, this makes it impossible. Much work is required to do so.

In the beginning, this work is concerned with removing undesirable qualities, traits and habits from the individuals' psyche. Working on rendering personality passive and awakening the activity of the growth of essence. Working on destroying negative emotions, internal considering: 'making accounts', identifying with the travesties of life, lying, self-justification, prejudice, etc, etc.

Then positive qualities must be developed in such a person: courage, truth, considering others, vision, sincerity, tenacity, active mentation and the ability to understand authentic esoteric wisdom.

However, developed essence has some very interesting characteristics. An individual with developed essence, through the application of esoteric Knowledge, is a very different kind of human being. This person will not be interested in social veneer, status or fame. Nor will this individual be swayed by political argument, 'plastic people' or the 'topic of the day'! Such an individual will only be ultimately interested in Truth! Such a person possesses real intelligence! Their aim will be that of inner-development here and now.

'Lying Kills Essence!'

Maurice Nicoll [55]

'Man's possibilities are very great. You cannot conceive a shadow of what man is capable of attaining. But nothing can be attained in sleep. In the consciousness of a sleeping man, his illusions, his 'dreams' are mixed with his reality. He lives in a subjective world and he can never escape from it. This is the reason he cannot make use of all the powers he possesses and why he lives in only a small part of himself!'

Gurdjieff [56]

DEVELOPED OR MATURED ESSENCE CONTINUED:

With the development of essence in an individual comes a heightened sense of themselves and a heightened sense of awareness. Everything becomes more vivid and more immediate: a new sense of perspective manifests.

Expanded essence brings many new insights about oneself and also about life in general. At this point it sometimes happens that an overlap occurs and one begins to have glimpses of the next level of consciousness possible for man.

OVERLAPS:

With heightened awareness and continued insights comes something entirely new … overlaps. That is, one begins to have flashes of the third state of consciousness, self-remembering or called 'the witnessing consciousness' by the Buddhists.

These flashes are a foretaste of things to come, if one is able to render this state permanent in ones psyche. <u>This is the purpose of all true esoteric work</u>!

THE WITNESSING CONSCIOUSNESS

The third state of consciousness possible for man is that of Self-Remembering or the 'Witnessing Consciousness'.

(Under 12 orders of laws) 'The Solar Consciousness'

With this state, where it is fixed in man, comes the expansion of consciousness and a new state of emotional cognition. This is the mystical state spoken of in Ages past, by mystics, monks and sages.

Essentially it cannot be described by words but some elements of this state can be mentioned, in order to give 'a fragrance' of what it entails.

- A general freedom from fear and 'fear-thinking'
- The perception of other people – is that they are asleep
- Surrounded by a 'bubble of silence' … everything more vivid!
- A new holistic perspective of oneself and the Cosmos
- A new link to the universe, one which cannot be described in words
- An awareness that one has found one of the great secrets of life
- We become fully aware of how mechanical people are in life
- Negative emotions disappear
- Appears in us in the beginning, as flashes of new consciousness
- One's cognitive abilities and perception change radically
- This is the third state of consciousness possible for man
- G. tells us that this state is our birthright – but now, must be worked for
- Thoughts still present but quite different
- There is a feeling that we are 'witnessing' life around us at a new level

OVERLAPS:

One begins to have glimpses of the fourth state of consciousness possible for man: objective consciousness!

OBJECTIVE CONSCIOUSNESS

THE FOURTH STATE OF CONSCIOUSNESS POSSIBLE FOR MAN

(Under 6 orders of laws) 'The Stellar Consciousness'

Objective consciousness is the result of long work, help and a tenacity difficult to describe. It is also the direct result of authentic esoteric wisdom applied as a catalyst, in order to achieve a level of intelligence and cognition unthinkable for most people.

With the advent of objective consciousness comes freedom for all negative emotions and states. Here enters the paradigm of positive emotions; where all centres function as an integrated whole … all centres function as <u>One Centre</u>! A direct linkage is forged between the two higher centres in a person and, the five lower centres.

With this development in a human being comes a whole raft of new powers and abilities: direct cognition of reality, telepathy, understanding symbols as powerful conduits of Knowledge and vision.

Key Concept: Direct vision of reality

COSMIC CONSCIOUSNESS

REFINED LEVEL OF FOURTH STATE OF CONSCIOUSNESS

(Under 3 orders of Laws) 'The Christ Consciousness'

Cosmic consciousness represents the levels 19 and 20 in 'the Science of Idiotism' which is used by certain high level Sufi Groups to this day. It is the closest a human being can develop in relation to the Absolute. The sphere of the Absolute or 'God' being that of level 21.

Christ was said by Gurdjieff to have achieved the level 19 and 20 on this scale of consciousness.

Christ consciousness means that the fine energy and cosmic intelligence, one step removed from the absolute, becomes manifest in the individual.

The individual is said to become 'a cell in the brain of the Absolute'. This level goes beyond the power of our mind to conceptualise. It is the highest level of Cosmic Truth and freedom possible for a man or a woman.

Powers include, travelling in time and space at will. Having a direct interface with the Absolute and the manifesting of laws from a higher cosmos in our cosmos. (The ability to create miracles.)

COSMIC LAWS GOVERNING LIFE ON EARTH

In order to understand the many cosmic laws surrounding Man, it will be first necessary to explain a little about the basic structuring of these laws and how they relate to us.

Here, we will look only at how those cosmic laws relate to Man's true inner psychology. The basic teaching from esoteric cosmology is that, <u>the more laws, the denser, the less intelligent, and less free a quantum is</u>! This also applies to man. The more laws a man 'places himself under', the less free he is. A man who follows the ordinary dictates of society, who neither questions nor doubts the veracity of its structure; who accepts it without any queries or deep Essence questioning, lives in the mechanical parts of his energy centres or chakras. By default, that is, by not making the necessary being efforts required by Great Nature, he is living mostly under 96 orders of laws (in the Superficial-Self) and sometimes under 48 orders of laws (in Personality) and occasionally, under 24 orders of laws (Essence).

So, In Effect We Have:

The Superficial-Self .... under 96 orders of laws
Personality.. under 48 orders of laws
Essence.. under 24 orders of laws
Real 'I' or 'Witnessing Consciousness'.................................. under 12 orders of laws
Objective Consciousness .... under 6 orders of laws
Cosmic Consciousness .... under 3 orders of laws
Absolute or God .... under one order of law

WHAT ONE MIGHT EXPECT TO ACHIEVE, INITIALLY, THROUGH THE STUDY AND APPLICATION OF ESOTERIC TEACHINGS. SOME, OR ALL, OF THE LIST BELOW:

UNDERSTANDING:

- Of one's life/one's inner-self
- Why we seem to fail in certain areas of life and succeed in others (The law of three and law of seven)
- Understanding other people …. esoteric psychology
- Understanding the modality of the cosmos and its different planes of interaction

DEVELOP NEW QUALITIES AND ABILITIES IN OURSELVES:

- Compassion/practice this first on animals
- Inner-calm
- Freedom from many old patterns and negative emotions
- Insight and emotional-clarity
- New powers of attention, memory and concentration are possible over time!
- The ability not to react to outer events

DEVELOP NEW SKILLS FOR LIFE:

Esotericism shows us that we should master as many life skills as possible – this expands our abilities, qualities, and practical aptitude.

VISION:

To see in another, not their outer form but their spirit. Also, to be able to put oneself in another's position.

To continually see others in terms of their outer-form is to see people in a one-dimensional fashion; when we should actually view them in a three-dimensional mode, in order to truly do them justice.

IDENTIFY FALSE-INTERESTS AND DROP THEM AS WE MATURE IN SPIRTIT!

THE POWER TO FREE OURSELVES FROM THE OPINIONS OF OTHERS – ESSENTIALLY TO FREE OURSELVES FROM OTHERS!

WORK ON OUR INNER-SELF … OUR ESSENCE:

In this work we begin to look at and develop the four natural powers of essence - 'the four powers of the Sphinx'.

- Humility
- Sincerity
- Courage
- Tenacity

WORK ON FREEING OURSELVES FROM THE POWER OF THE SUPERFICIAL-SELF/FALSE-EGO or FALSE-PERSONALITY:

This work involves self-observation and taking 'mental photographs' of ourselves, and sometimes of others, over time – giving us a new vision and understanding of our own inner mechanisms and how the false-ego continually blocks our real progress and development!

WORK ON CREATING A FUSION BETWEEN OUR MIND AND EMOTIONS:

… which produces a new force. This force is then utilised for higher learning and a deeper understanding of ourselves and the cosmos we live in.

FORMULATING ONE'S AIM/S AND ONE'S TRUE LIFE PATH:

The absorbing of esoteric materials and knowledge will often enable an individual to formulate their 'life-plan' and aims more effectively.

UNDERSTANDING <u>THE REAL NATURE OF OUR OWN INNER-BEING</u>:

And how it manifests: Essence, Personality and the False-Ego. (See diagram for details of this actual structure.)

LEARN TO THINK IN A NEW WAY … LEARN TO THINK FOR YOURSELF!

CREATE 'MAGNETIC CENTRE' IN ONESELF:

Learning <u>to value</u> real Knowledge and keeping it alive in oneself at all times.

BROADENING ONE'S INNER PSYCHOLOGY BEYOND NARROW SELF-INTEREST:

Using Karma Yoga as a tool to broaden one's emotional field and core cognition: the cognition of the inner-meaning of things, people and events.

FINDING REAL MEANING IN LIFE:

The very first objective for every human being is to obtain meaning in his or her life. The difficulty for people is that, as one progresses in life, meaning changes, it does not remain the same. What held meaning for us in our early life will no longer hold meaning in later life. One must find meaning which is unchanging! With meaning given by ordinary life; work, education, friends, relationships, hobbies – this is not possible. This happens because our relationship to these things changes over time. All are incredibly mutable, morphic and in constant flux; there is no stable datum in ordinary things!

SOME QUOTATIONS FROM WORK MATERIALS

DESTINY VERSUS THE LAW OF ACCIDENT

RESISTANCE FORCE IN US

'... When a person makes as his aim change of himself, his chief-feature stands up as second force to resist him. But people do not see that they have second force in themselves. They see it always as outside of themselves.'

Maurice Nicoll [57]

THE FLOWER AND THE STONE

'When the great teacher and martyr El-Hallai was exposed to the crowd, convicted of apostasy, and heresy, he showed no evidence of pain when his hands were publicly chopped-off. When the crowd threw stones which inflected great wounds, he made no sign. One of his friends, a Sufi teacher, approached and struck him with a flower... Mansur screamed as if in torture. He did this in order to show that he could not be hurt by anything done by those who thought that they were doing right. But the merest touch from someone who knew, like him, that he was unjustly accused and condemned was more hurtful to him than any torture.

Mansur and his Sufi friends, helpless though they were in the face of such tyranny, are remembered for that lesson; while their torturers are forgotten.

As he was dying, Mansur said: "The people of the world try to do good, I recommend you to seek something of which the smallest part is worth more than all 'goodness': THE KNOWLEDGE OF WHAT IS TRUE ... TRUE SCIENCE!"

Idres Shah [58]

FAST ASLEEP EVEN WHILE AWAKE

'To change your being, to raise its level, you must begin to think in a new way. And all the

115

ideas given you again and again in the Work are to furnish you with the means of <u>thinking in a new way</u>. The idea that <u>man is asleep</u> is a new idea, as is the personal application of it – meaning that <u>you are asleep</u>. The whole general idea that a man can <u>evolve in life</u>, and is created to do so, is again a new idea.

The ideas of the Work conduct very great force when they are taken in and become part of your inner thinking. But life-ideas drain you of force. They make you identify with life and all its events. Life drains people. The work ideas protect you from life and help you create more force. They prevent life from 'eating' you – that is, the Moon (from receiving your force).'

Maurice Nicoll [59]

THE GREATER FREEDOM AND THE LESSER FREEDOM

'Freedom leads to freedom. Those are the first words of truth. You do not know what is truth because you do not know what freedom is. All the truth that you know today is only "truth" in quotation marks. <u>There is another truth, but it is not theoretical: it cannot be expressed in words. Only those who have realised it in themselves can understand that truth</u>.

The freedom I speak about is the freedom that is the goal of all schools, all religions, of all times. And, in truth, that this freedom can be a very great one.

Everyone wishes for that freedom and even strives for it: but it can never be attained without the first kind of freedom, that I will call the lesser freedom.

The greater freedom is liberation of ourselves from all influences acting outside ourselves. The lesser freedom is the liberation of ourselves from all influences acting within us.

You must understand that you cannot begin with freedom – freedom is the goal, the aim. People say that God created man free. That is a great misunderstanding. Freedom cannot be given to anyone – even by our all loving Creator himself. God has given to man the biggest thing he can – that is, the possibility to become free. The desire for freedom exists in every man worthy of the name – but people are stupid, and they think they can have outer freedom without inner freedom. All evil comes from this stupidity. Unless we desire, first to be free from our inner enemies, we shall only go from bad to worse.'

Gurdjieff [60]

THE CHAIN OF TRANSMISSION

So, one can see from the previous pages alone, that there is much involved here. However, we must start at the beginning, regardless of who we are in the external world. At the outset, there are three main stages in this work and people normally progress through these stages according to their inner-development.

- Being inspired by the concept of esotericism
- A sense of urgency develops
- Conscious efforts

In the beginning, the stage of being inspired is of deep significance. Being inspired acts as a catalyst for further study and Work. Usually being inspired means being inspired by another person or individual in the Work itself or, by a figurehead in esotericism from the past. It is important to keep this inspiration alive in us, otherwise the initial impressions which set us in motion begin to fade and we remain static and do not move forward.

We need to learn to take in impressions (this can be esoteric materials) and transform them upwards in an ascending scale, in ourselves. This requires a small amount of explaining. Normally impressions enter our organism through 'the top story' of our 'machine' - the head; they enter at the level of vibration calibrated by esotericism at H48. However, depending how we *take them in*, we can transform them to much finer vibrations of H24 and H12 … even H6!

What this actually means in real terms is that, we must not take esoteric Knowledge at the same level as a novel, a newspaper or an academic paper. Esoteric Knowledge must be pondered or 'digested' slowly and in a totally different way to conventional materials.

This process of taking in impressions consciously will not happen all at once but over time. Esoteric Knowledge unlike terrestrial knowledge or information is *loaded with a fine energy!* But, if one approaches this Knowledge in the same way as terrestrial knowledge, there is no transfer of these fine impressions or fine energies.

The Chain-of-Transmission exists for this purpose; to facilitate the transmission of esoteric Wisdom, which carries these fine energies or foods for Man's inner-world. This principle of transmission simply means the projection of authentic *Living Knowledge* into the World. This esoteric Knowledge comes to us from *the conscious inner circle of humanity* and is designed to aid us in our development as human beings on this planet.

This does not happen mechanically but requires effort on our part and a specific recognition from us, regarding its value and significance.

Esoteric workshops serve in part to facilitate this transmission of unique Wisdom. For workshop dates and venues please contact Mr McKeaney on UK cell phone 07500 860835 or josephmckeaney@hotmail.com.

Postscript

- Recapitulation of Principles
- The Inner-State of Modern Man
- 'Education', Modern Medicine and Science

1. The themes mentioned in this manual constitute a very different and radical approach to life: society, human nature, man's inner psychology and how we view these subjects. Gurdjieff tells us that esoteric teachings which deal primarily with <u>our true inner potential,</u> do not come to us from ordinary men, nor for that matter from ordinary society. He tells us that our ordinary mind-set and all of the modern academia around us cannot discover this ancient science through modern methodology and research. This, again, because of contemporary man's cognitive level – as a rule, he tells us, we can only see our own level and those levels below us. <u>Esotericism, he recounts, comes to us from a much higher level than ourselves .... higher-mind!</u>

Generally speaking, from the point of view of higher mind, we lack the cognitive range required to explore authentic esoteric teachings. These teachings, of such importance to modern life, are positioned <u>just outside the cognitive level of modern peoples – there are, of course, exceptions to this rule</u>! In order for us to approach esoteric teachings today, <u>we need a very specific preparation, which</u> <u>includes the removal of filters from our psyche – also known as programming</u>! (Modern man is a highly conditioned entity.)

Further, and most regrettably for contemporary man, many elements in modern society, such as our contemporary 'education', now only serve to increase our mistrust and misunderstanding of this ancient science; so much so, that most people today have developed a very cynical and warped attitude to same! The chief modality of modern 'education' is to focus minds and to some degree emotions, on technology, 'scientific progress', status, consumer culture, ownership, fame, 'cultural activities', to worship 'education' itself etc, etc.

Regrettably, this narrow modality leads to a host of secondary effects in modern peoples, such as: a banal competitive mind-set, narrow self-interest, a muted cognitive ability, cloned opinions, trite intellectual attitudes, 'profit at any cost', a 'them and us mentality', gross ignorance in relation to world affairs, naivety, emotional immaturity, a lack of inter-personal skills, etc, etc. <u>We now place all our hopes for the future in status, fame, material possessions, property, wealth, scientific</u>

discoveries, new technologies to make life easy – thus ever increase comfort and convenience! Contemporary man has no idea how naive these hopes are. Inner-growth cannot take place in 'a comfort-zone' – it is necessary to 'step outside' that 'comfort-zone'!

Gurdjieff tells us that, although we are not aware of it, the state of contemporary man is now critical: internally, in terms of his Being-development and also externally, in terms of trite societal structuring and our banal 'cultural activities'. Social structures and people's critical faculties now lack substance and veracity. People have now become supremely suggestible and as G. Explains: 'will believe any old tale'. The masses subscribe to a long list of false societal structures and fake 'educational' modalities! To convince people otherwise means you 'don the devil's mask' and become their 'enemy for life'! An increase in one's cognitive level means that we begin to perceive

all of this in 'technicolour' ... we can no longer hide from it!

One of the most interesting features of all of this is that the reader will often agree but exempt him or herself from the equation! It is very difficult for the modern individual to accept that their socioscape is so corrupt, corrosive, banal and inept. The 'modern mind-set' is highly conditioned and is so powerfully identified with these very same false societal structures and banal 'cultural activities', that we often witness strong aggressive reactions to 'the very nature of esoteric thought'.

It is not possible for modern peoples to live in a contemporary society and not be subject to these highly spiritually corrosive and banal influences! Only through the use of exceptional modalities from outside of society can man resist these very powerful and omnipresent pressures!

We see the tenets of various original religious teachings, set forth in writings, the primary aim of which was to help people resist these narrow and damaging societal influences. Too well did the original founders know the danger of these harmful and mechanical activities and beliefs. Unfortunately, many people no longer follow the primary principles of their religion, plus, most religions have become diluted in nature and no longer carry their former power and cohesion. Religion for the most part has lost its core! The word religion means to re-align; to re-align our thinking, our actions and in real terms – our cognitive ability or perceptions.

2. The Inner State of Modern Man: G. tells us, we all presume that we are conscious and that people generally possess integrity and a Conscience. This is, in reality, very far from the truth. Our programming creates in us a wrong picture of reality and of society – we cannot lose the 'emotional-picture' we hold of a healthy, vibrant

and cohesive society. According to Gurdjieff, society is very sick but appears on the surface to be quite healthy and vigorous. With a deeper inspection; a change in our cognitive level, we find something quite different – a civilisation of sleeping people struggling through life, suffering, lying, manipulating each other, exploiting where possible an already embattled planet, engaging in warfare, creating weapons of mass destruction, governments deceiving their own populations and through all of this, everyone still trying to manage a smile.

In reality, <u>it should be the goal of modern people, to have real integrity,</u> strong objective principles, reliability and a Conscience! Ordinarily, man has no true integrity and everything flows from this, because the level of our integrity has a direct co-relationship to that of the level of our Being!

Normally, people 'go with the flow' in life, in real terms this means that if an opportunity arises, for instance, to make a large profit from some venture or enterprise; people will often choose this sizeable profit <u>over their friends and sometimes even their family members</u>!

<u>The principle of integrity means not exploiting others and, not allowing others to exploit you</u>! It is a very important principle to avoid in any way the exploitation of others and equally important, not to allow the reverse; it is a major karmic issue which is vastly underestimated. <u>Keeping this principle creates a powerful karmic field for the individual</u>!

Now, of course, this does not mean that a person will exploit every time; <u>this is thinking in extremes</u>! However, it is safe to say, that this kind of behaviour is very often prevalent in society today! This is an example of how man's psyche has degraded and how he experiences no Essence-shame in relation to his behaviour.

When a person behaves in this way, they will 'rationalise', 'smoke-screen' and generally 'fudge the issues'. Fudging the issues is now a major facet of modern society, and <u>is a core form of lying</u>!

This brings us to lying in modern man –

Lying in our modern societies has become endemic, so much so, that now we see it strongly featured in most professionals; lawyers, estate agents, the police, the judiciary, builders, garage mechanics, etc.

Why do people not react very strongly to this <u>toxic lying</u> in societal structures and organisations? Why is there such widespread acceptance?

The reason for this, is that people themselves all lie and so much so, that, it is now 'an accepted part of society'; we have arrived at a stage where we simply accept it as part of life – something we have to deal with on a day to day basis! <u>It has become endemic</u>!

'Man follows the path of least resistance; to the pressure of outside forces.'

Gurdjieff [66]

Lying in society has become so toxic and prevalent in all areas of life, that it now has a major impact and corrosive effect on all the individual members of society. Nobody today, escapes the indirect impact of lying in our culture; our culture could be called '<u>a culture of lies</u>' without any exaggeration or malice!

3. Education: It might be construed by the reader, from what has been written in this manual, that the writer is completely against modern 'education', science and modern medicine – this is, of course, a completely wrong picture of things.

All of the above are slowly evolving and there are many valuable elements to all three of these disciplines.

However, currently, there exists a <u>strange and bizarre fear</u> of criticising these three prominent facets of our society. With others, there is such identification and also 'emotional investment' in some or all of these, that to criticise any of them is now taboo and taken as a personal insult or a direct attack on them, themselves!

One of the vital esoteric principles informs us that, in order for an individual to be balanced and function in accordance with our 'original blueprint', we must always have in our inner make-up three centres working in harmony; emotional centre, intellectual centre and, instinctive/moving centre. Unfortunately, modern day people have no concept of the centres or chakras in Man and therefore, are very much unaware that <u>modern 'education' only focuses on the intellect</u>! In particular, <u>the emotional function and inner make-up of the student is never taken into account</u>! (Each child is different!)

That is, the students' qualities, abilities and traits are never considered in a proper fashion – it is as if, intellectual study of various subjects, learning mostly by rote, with a little sports activities and drama thrown in 'for good measure' will address 'the whole person' in the student? The emotional-side of the student is starved! <u>The student is seen as 'a circus animal' to be trained </u>and the students themselves <u>are never properly considered or consulted</u>!

In the vast majority of cases one cannot develop strong qualities or real traits and abilities through the medium of today's school syllabus. It is just an illusion. In most cases, students leave their 'education', including higher 'education' with no training of their emotional side and so possess a weak 'emotional field', unable to think for themselves and, lacking real confidence – which comes from finding solutions to real life problems and surmounting them, and unable to form mature and stable relations with others.

Students leave with the same 'blot' in their 'emotional-field', and it is called narrow self-interest! Thus, the ability to give genuine help to others, without some kind of payment, is often null and void! All potential spiritual aspirations are now replaced by the powerful compulsion to acquire 'a job' or 'a career', and, of course, an insatiable interest in such things as science, gadgets, computers, new software or 'apps', and another certificate from 'higher education', which is very often never used!

There is also a further most important facet to be addressed in all of this, and is that of <u>meaning in one's life</u>.

The emotional part of a human being is connected to the deepest part of our make-up; the Essence or Spirit of the person. Essence can grow and mature only through the reception of Truth, that is, through the reception of quality impressions and wisdom of a high order. Essence cannot grow and mature from the same knowledge and information which is sufficient for Personality; i.e. the knowledge and information which modern day students consume.

Essence, it must be remembered, is <u>that which is real in an individual</u>, and <u>Personality is 'the mask' or that which is cloned from our societal influences</u>!

Thus, with contemporary 'education' Personality grows and expands but, at the expense of Essence in the person. The impressions and knowledge found in most contemporary schools are too coarse and lack veracity, and so do not provide food for Essence to grow. <u>Essence, in effect, becomes trapped by Personality, which takes over 'the driver's seat' and Essence becomes the passive, 'back seat passenger'</u> as it were!

Essence requires a different type of food, in order to grow; <u>it requires meaning</u> beyond the theories of science and the platitudes of religion. Only <u>a living Knowledge</u> can provide nourishment for the Essence, a wisdom that carries very fine 'hydrogens' or energies; these fine energies 'feed' the 'abandoned' spiritual part of Man, but these <u>fine energies are not present in the materials, mind-set and modus operandi of contemporary schools and colleges</u>!

Without these fine energies being distilled from life and tempered into his Being; <u>Man remains a 'thinking animal' and not an intelligent Being</u>! Gurdjieff explains that the difference between an enlightened person and an individual, who has not developed, is greater than the chasm between say, a man and a monkey in terms of qualities, abilities and cognitive intelligence!

In reality, man is a highly complex and sophisticated cosmic unit and is capable of extrapolating from his biosphere, highly refined energy/matters; which are ever present and plentiful – these fine energies permeate into our plane of existence from higher cosmic levels and provide us with the opportunity to develop from a Planetary Being into a Cosmic Being! This is not understood by modern science but was the subject of ancient sciences of the Earth, including that of authentic ancient Alchemy.

We will revisit this most vital of subjects in future volumes; we will look at the great contemporary thinkers, who have had the courage to point out the many weaknesses in our modern 'education' system – such as John Dewy, Jean Piaget, Paolo Freire, Krishnamurti and Osho.

Modern Medicine

Obviously the subject of modern medicine encompasses very many fields and expertise in many spheres: here we will mainly focus on that aspect of contemporary medicine, which is referred to as pharmaceutical medicine.

Pharmaceutical Medicine:

Esotericism warns us about the use of pharmaceutical drugs. There are many sides to this phenomenon. Here, I will keep it brief and outline some of those dangers which should be obvious to all:

Over-prescription of drugs in modern society
- Side effects occurring with almost all modern drugs
- 5,000 deaths in the U.K each year, from prescription drugs alone
- An estimated 10,000 deaths from medical mistakes and malpractice!
- The reliance on a chemical solution to problems which could be better treated by other means, e.g. exercise, saunas, massage and a healthy diet
- Addiction: Ever increasing numbers of ordinary people are becoming addicted to prescription drugs
- The emerging mind-set which holds that an 'instant fix' must be available
- Invasive surgical practices which are often unnecessary
- We also have a situation, where the authorities themselves estimate that as

many as 10,000 people die in the U.K each year from medical errors and misdiagnosis of their illness/condition

- Many doctors, although they know the side effects of certain drugs quite well, will not inform their patients about these side effects!
- Further, quite a ludicrous situation arises when a patient suffers clear side effects from a drug prescribed from their doctor, and when the patient outlines these side effects at their local surgery/clinic, their doctor often dismisses them as not being related to the drug

We now have a situation where vaccines, with dangerous contents, are given to a wider and wider segment of the population; causing human diseases which were not even heard of a hundred years ago. People, not having scientific knowledge with regard to the actual content and make up of these vaccines, take them and allow their children to take them en masse!

Much false information is spread in the media about these vaccines and their effectiveness. The truth about vaccines has been so well hidden behind a 'smoke screen' of lies and half-truths, that the public are totally confused. Every now and then, the authorities, through the cynical use of the media, create deliberate fear among the masses in order to achieve compliance with their wishes and corporate plans. (Suggestibility of the masses.)

Science:

Due to modern 'education' science has become the new religion. People now worship science more than anything else in contemporary culture!

New discoveries in science have seen advances in medicine, surgical techniques, technology and communications. It has also revolutionised transport and food production with the modern methods of storing food and mechanised food production.

People now, in general, look to science with all their hope for the future. There is no longer any deep inspirational interest and dedication to the spiritual quest!

This 'love affair' with science was foreseen by the ancients and was called the 'Kali-Yuga': the age of stone and metal, many thousands of years before it actually manifested on Earth.

Esoteric teachings have warned not to place too much 'emotional capital' in science. Outwardly, Man may be changing over centuries and many things have improved, but inwardly Man's cognitive ability or Being has dwindled. This fact, of

Man's Being having 'dwarfed' is unknown to modern science and is likely to remain so – science actually believes that Man's cognitive ability has grown! (Intellectual level has increased but cognitive ability decreased.)

This, of course, means that Man can use vast amounts of information at his disposal in ordinary life; however cognitive ability means to see deeper into life and deeper into the nature of things – something intellectual capacity cannot do! For instance, it is mere 'child's-play' to demonstrate this: Man cannot discern the concept of his own inner-potential through any intellectual means.

Modern science now is 'in the dark' about so many vital issues, that one might be excused for 'lifting one's eyebrows' very high indeed – once one realises just how much contemporary science has failed to grasp! Contemporary people cannot see this situation since their cognitive range is moulded by this same thinking!

In the section on education we mentioned one such omission or 'blind spot'; that of Man as a transformational entity – with the hidden capacity to transform coarse energies ('hydrogens') into finer energies. Man, by way of digestion of food H768, the intake of impressions H48 and air H192, produces a relatively high 'hydrogen' – H si 12! (Sex energy). The key to this transformation is that it all happens mechanically – there is no conscious input on the part of the person! (A process engineered by nature not Man!)

This H si 12 can be further transformed into even finer energies; however, this requires a Knowledge and insight (Esoteric Science) that contemporary science has no access to! Contemporary science does not even understand how these energies function in Man and how they can be developed. The key to this further development and all the subsequent ramifications, which we will deal with later in a future volume, is that it is a conscious act; in other words, it requires specific conscious efforts informed by a specialist Knowledge. It cannot happen by itself. (Man's inner-development is a conscious process!)

What is most astounding of all is that this refinement of energy in Man is very easily explained! There are, of course, different levels of refinement! The first stages of refinement in Man can be seen happening in ordinary society!

In the practice of tai chi, chi-gung and certain martial arts, this transformation of energy is both the principle, practice and goal! Chi is increased in the individual! (Chi is a form of refined energy; in esotericism – 'hydrogen' 96!)

For example the martial art called Lu-hop-bat-fat, otherwise known as Lu style, is based on the development and use of 'hard-chi' or internal force, which can be projected outwards in combat. This type of internal-chi is easily demonstrated by the practitioner breaking house building bricks; with different blows from the hands and feet!

Modern science has no explanation for this type of energy and often puts it down to 'the intense focus of the mind'. It is very easy to demonstrate that this cannot be so: for if one were to invite any person to try and break a single house brick with their hands (using only a blow), even those with great concentration and focus of the mind, it would prove impossible – because 'hydrogen 96' would be missing! This energy *has to be cultivated and increased in the body* before it may be used in the fashion described. A person becomes *charged like a battery* and then, with the conditioning and hardening of the hands; one can dispatch house bricks at will! (For those who are cynical – the conditioning and hardening of the hands alone will prove insufficient and, success will depend on the cultivation of chi, using breathing techniques which have been handed down from ancient times.)

The brick or piece of wood is broken by the martial artist by means of this H 96, it is discharged in the blow *through an act of intention;* in this way it is possible, in time, to break five or six bricks in a stack – awesome internal power!

Science does not recognise this energy called chi because it has no authentic understanding of how the 'human-machine' can produce it? So, there is much that contemporary science just simply ignores – when it cannot comprehend!

Similarly, in the practice of tai chi and chi-gung, the practitioner produces, over time, a similar type of chi but one that can also be used to heal others. This is called a 'soft-chi'. There are branches of chi-gung, which are totally dedicated to this 'soft-chi': self-healing and healing others!

Neither is this healing energy or hydrogen understood by our contemporary science? Our contemporary science has simply avoided the whole subject!

Such is the veracity of this energy that it can be readily demonstrated even in a 'controlled environment'. Chi-gung masters have the power to remove sickness from the body or even a headache; at close quarters, simply by using their *external-force* and 'pulling' the negative energy out of the brain. This exact incident once happened to me personally, upon entering my chi-gung class as per usual – my teacher noticed (cognitively) that I had a headache and proceeded to remove it skillfully using only *external-force:* to my great relief!

There is so much in our contemporary world that modern science cannot explain; this was the principle reason Gurdjieff set out on a voyage of discovery, in order to clarify for himself all those issues which puzzled him and, the unexplained *super-human phenomena* he had witnessed in his youth!

In the end, he ultimately penetrated what esotericism calls *the Greater Mysteries;* of time, Space and of higher Being! He fulfilled his life in a way that perhaps, even he, had never dreamed of! The paradigm of *homo-superior* became a living reality for him!

Gurdjieff had originally formally studied science and religion in an effort to find answers to the questions which he said 'gave him no peace' and 'gnawed at him continuously'. He could not find the answers he sought in these disciplines and eventually *intuited* that the answers he sought could only be found in the wisdom societies of ancient civilisations that once existed on the Earth. It was only to be found through making contact with an unbroken line of these wisdom schools; in this case, he made contact with the Sarmoung Brotherhood, in Central Asia. This was to be the pivotal encounter.

Gurdjieff's life story and his restless search for Truth, is in itself, a powerful testament to the futility of seeking authentic life solutions and Truth in secular society and within contemporary science and religion in particular!

We can only find at best traces or fragments of Truth in our culture or society, all of which point to *an underground stream*; a hidden esoteric tradition which stands just outside our cognitive level and also outside of mainstream society!

Gurdjieff's life story is a skilful anecdotal narrative; illustrating to the reader how he himself, met with all the usual spiritual paths in life and found them to be defunct; in other words, he could not use them as practical methods of genuine inner-development! In real terms he is saving us time by saying; look I have tried all the usual methodologies and spiritual paths to be found in life, they do not work – no need to repeat and replicate my search and mistakes – there is a hidden Path, one which is a Core Teaching and from which all of the other lesser paths originate: they are but 'leaves fallen from the esoteric tree.'

We will continue our deep exploration of the core principles and ideas, of this most ancient of our Earth's sciences – esotericism, in volume two of this series.

Bibliography

1. Sufi saying - Origins unknown
2. Lau Tzu from the Tao Te Ching by Stephen Hodge
3. A Nervo – Mexican poet
4. Chinese proverb – Origins unknown
5. Quote from Gurdjieff; taken from Maurice Nicoll's Psychological Commentaries
6. Maurice Nicoll - Psychological Commentaries
7. From the Rituals of the Golden Dawn by Israel Regardie
8. P.D. Ouspensky – In Search of the Miraculous
9. P.D. Ouspensky - In Search of the Miraculous
10. Maurice Nicoll - Psychological Commentaries
11. Quote from Gurdjieff – taken from Maurice Nicoll: Psychological Commentaries
12. Maurice Nicoll – Psychological Commentaries
13. I. Ching - Origins unknown
14. Rumi - Origins unknown
15. Maurice Nicoll – Psychological Commentaries
16. The writer
17. Erich Fromm - 'The Essential Fromm'
18. Earl Nightingale – Origins unknown
19. Maurice Nicoll – Psychological Commentaries
20. Sayed Najmuddin - Way of the Sufi by Idres Shah
21. Hadrat Chisti – Way of the Sufi by Idres Shah
22. Thomas Szasz - Origins unknown
23. Noam Chomsky - Manufacturing Consent
24. Osho - Wisdom of the Sands volume 2
25. Saadi of Shiraz – Shah
26. Erich Fromm - 'The Essential Fromm'
27. Gurdjieff – All and Everything
28. Gurdjieff – All and Everything
29. Gurdjieff – All and Everything
30. Gurdjieff – All and Everything
31. Erich Fromm – 'The Essential Fromm'
32. Erich Fromm – 'The Essential Fromm'
33. P.D. Ouspensky - In Search of the Miraculous
34. Gurdjieff – taken from Maurice Nicoll: Psychological Commentaries

35. Osho – Wisdom of the Sands. Volume 2
36. Maurice Nicoll - Psychological Commentaries
37. Maurice Nicoll - Psychological Commentaries
38. Maurice Nicoll - Psychological Commentaries
39. Patanjali (Indian sage) – Origins unknown
40. Maurice Nicoll - Psychological Commentaries
41. Gurdjieff – Life is Real only then, when 'I am'
42. Maurice Nicoll - Psychological Commentaries
43. Maurice Nicoll - Psychological Commentaries
44. Maurice Nicoll - Psychological Commentaries
45. Rumi – from The Essential Rumi
46. Gurdjieff – Views from the Real World
47. Osho - Wisdom of the Sands. Volume 2
48. Maurice Nicoll - Psychological Commentaries
49. Maurice Nicoll - Psychological Commentaries
50. P.D. Ouspensky - Conscience – The Search for Truth
51. Gurdjieff – Views from the Real World
52. Maurice Nicoll - Psychological Commentaries
53. Maurice Nicoll - Psychological Commentaries
54. P.D. Ouspensky - In Search of the Miraculous
55. Maurice Nicoll - Psychological Commentaries
56. Gurdjieff – Views from the Real World
57. Maurice Nicoll - Psychological Commentaries
58. Idres Shah - Way of the Sufi
59. Maurice Nicoll - Psychological Commentaries
60. Gurdjieff – Life is Real only then when 'I am'
61. Gurdjieff – Views from the Real World

Esoteric Psychology

The True Psychology of Man
<u>A1</u>

Essence feeds on Truth and can only grow and mature through the reception of Truth. Personality feeds on half-truths and complex lies. The False-Ego feeds on arguments, prejudice, fantasy and negativity. It also feeds on the trite approval of others and superficial praise.

Essence is surrounded by personality; encased or imprisoned (key phrase – 'genie in a bottle') by personality and personality in turn, is often encased by the false ego ... in effect, the persons' real self and real potential are unrealised. (Embryonic man.) Personality and the False-Ego are usually the active force in ordinary man!

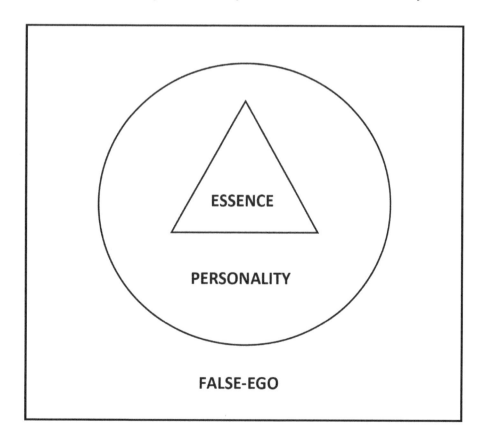

DIAGRAM DEPICTING ESSENCE AS ACTIVE FORCE IN THE INDIVIDUAL:
A2

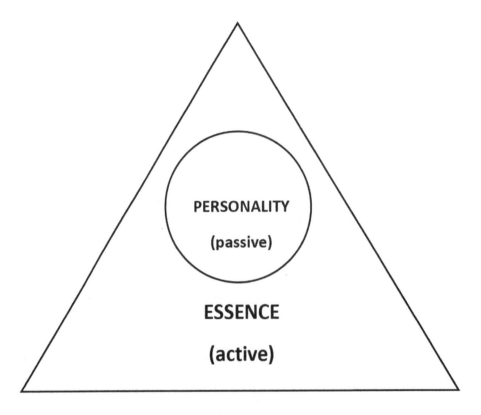

This is how our inner psychology should be: notice false-personality is absent from the diagram. (Essence is under 24 orders of laws.)

Personality has become secondary. Essence has become the active force in the Individual – (Key phrase – 'increased inner freedom'). This achievement of balanced functions in man is a result of inner-work and new Knowledge: it can however be reversed through the corrosive effect of outer life and mechanical societal and cultural influences. It is easy to fall back to the former position, without help and increased incremental inner-work. Remember, outer-life and mechanical cultural influences 'drive personality' and these factors never sleep! (Rendering Essence active is called the second reversal.)

KEY ELEMENTS OF PERSONALITY

CANNOT DISTINGUISH DIFFERENT LEVELS OF KNOWLEDGE
(I.E. CANNOT PERCEIVE THE EXISTANCE OF HIGHER-LEARNING)
(All learning is superficial – automatic reason – all knowledge is borrowed)

A3

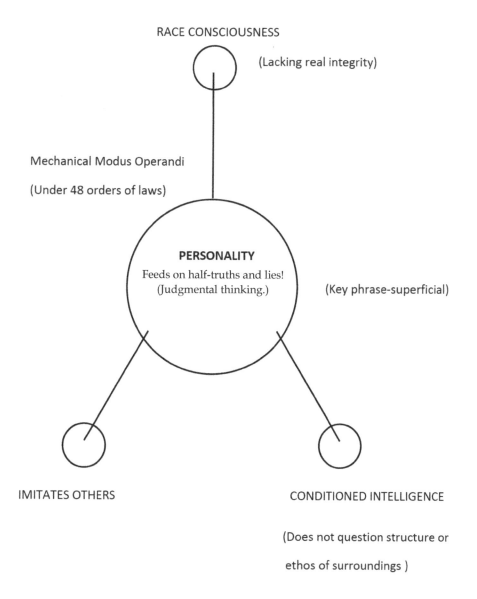

RACE CONSCIOUSNESS

(Lacking real integrity)

Mechanical Modus Operandi

(Under 48 orders of laws)

PERSONALITY
Feeds on half-truths and lies!
(Judgmental thinking.)

(Key phrase-superficial)

IMITATES OTHERS

CONDITIONED INTELLIGENCE

(Does not question structure or

ethos of surroundings)

KEY ELEMENTS OF THE FALSE – EGO

DOMINANT TRAIT ... NARROW SELF-INTEREST

(Causes suffering for the individual and also friends – 96 orders of laws)
A4

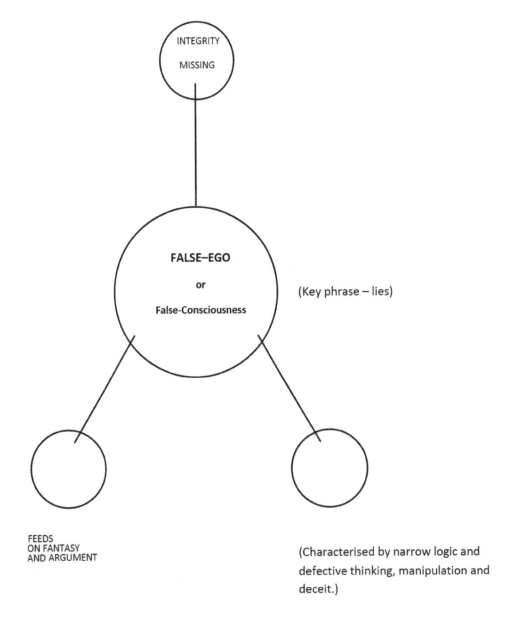

INTEGRITY

MISSING

FALSE–EGO

or

False-Consciousness

(Key phrase – lies)

FEEDS
ON FANTASY
AND ARGUMENT

(Characterised by narrow logic and defective thinking, manipulation and deceit.)

ACQUIRED OR FALSE - CONSCIENCE:

A5

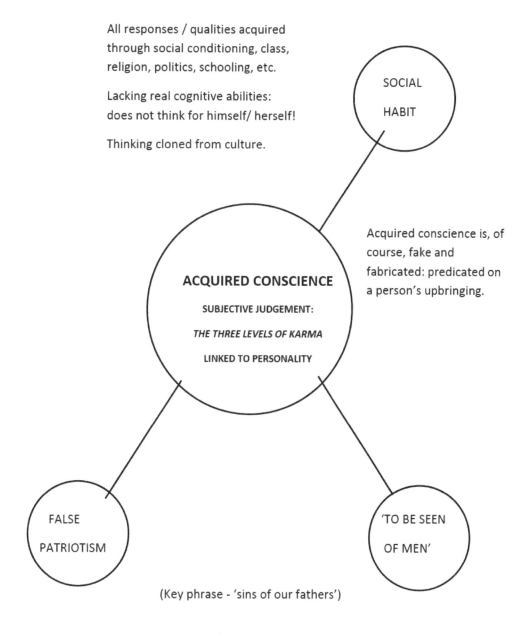

All responses / qualities acquired through social conditioning, class, religion, politics, schooling, etc.

Lacking real cognitive abilities: does not think for himself/ herself!

Thinking cloned from culture.

SOCIAL

HABIT

ACQUIRED CONSCIENCE

SUBJECTIVE JUDGEMENT:

THE THREE LEVELS OF KARMA

LINKED TO PERSONALITY

Acquired conscience is, of course, fake and fabricated: predicated on a person's upbringing.

FALSE

PATRIOTISM

'TO BE SEEN

OF MEN'

(Key phrase - 'sins of our fathers')

KEY ELEMENTS OF CONSCIENCE

NO LONGER PRESENT IN ORDINARY MAN
(REPLACED BY ACQUIRED-CONSCIENCE!)

A6

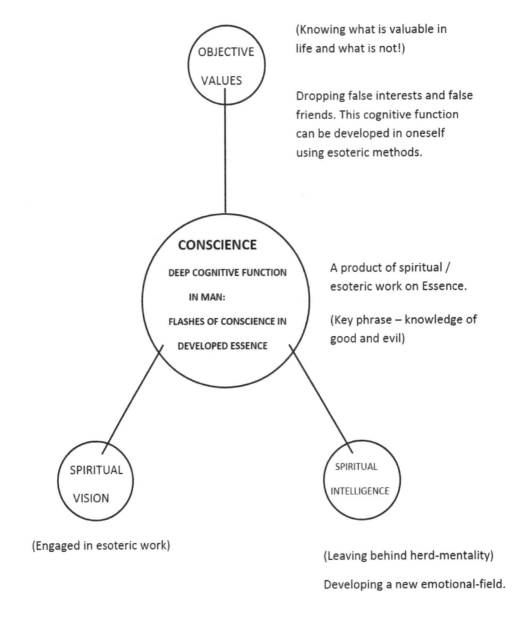

(Knowing what is valuable in life and what is not!)

Dropping false interests and false friends. This cognitive function can be developed in oneself using esoteric methods.

OBJECTIVE VALUES

CONSCIENCE

DEEP COGNITIVE FUNCTION

IN MAN:

FLASHES OF CONSCIENCE IN

DEVELOPED ESSENCE

A product of spiritual / esoteric work on Essence.

(Key phrase – knowledge of good and evil)

SPIRITUAL VISION

SPIRITUAL INTELLIGENCE

(Engaged in esoteric work)

(Leaving behind herd-mentality)

Developing a new emotional-field.

KEY ELEMENTS OF DEVELOPED ESSENCE

THE ABILITY TO PLACE ONESELF IN THE POSITION OF ANOTHER

(NEW COGNITIVE ABILITIES)

A7

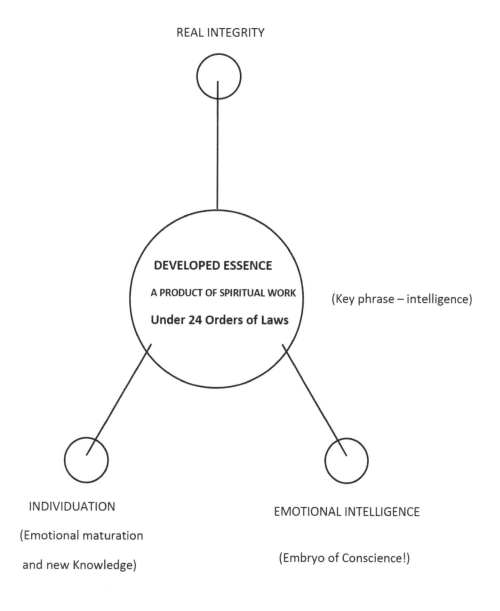

REAL INTEGRITY

DEVELOPED ESSENCE

A PRODUCT OF SPIRITUAL WORK

Under 24 Orders of Laws

(Key phrase – intelligence)

INDIVIDUATION

(Emotional maturation

and new Knowledge)

EMOTIONAL INTELLIGENCE

(Embryo of Conscience!)